Praise for *Two Beats Ahead*

"*Two Beats Ahead* is the first of its kind—a book that turns on its ear the popular myth that business and the arts are at odds with each other. There is so much we can learn from musicians about innovation and creativity in business, and in this groundbreaking and riveting book, Panos A. Panay and R. Michael Hendrix show us exactly what we're missing."

—Amy Cuddy, social psychologist and bestselling author of *Presence*

"I have always believed that the best outcomes in life come from the discipline of business combined with the chaos of art. All successful musicians are entrepreneurs and all great business leaders are artists. In *Two Beats Ahead*, Panay and Hendrix prove it. This is a must-read if you want to enjoy finding the path of least resistance to the dream you are chasing!"

—Kevin O'Leary, *Shark Tank* investor and chairman, O'Shares ETFs

"At its heart, this is a book about the creative journey. While the main ingredient is music, it is spiced with entrepreneurship, leadership, and design, and served through engaging stories. The result is one that will be of great inspiration to anyone looking to expand the reach of their creativity."

—Tim Brown, chair of IDEO and author of *Change by Design*

"For a long time, researchers have known that musical intelligence can awaken the nonlinear whole mind to healing, creativity, and innovation. This book is a roadmap for innovators, entrepreneurs, and those seeking new avenues for exploring and reimagining the future evolution of human consciousness and its infinite possibilities."

—Deepak Chopra, MD

"How we perceive the world is the key to how we act in the world. Based on their course at Berklee, Panay and Hendrix show that a musician's perspective, much like a designer's perspective, can unlock inspiration and innovation, no matter who you are."

—David Kelley, founder of IDEO and the Stanford d.school

"This book is not just about innovation. It may be the most provocative and thoughtful business book of its time, an approach to managing through the cacophony of fifty years of disruption."

—Jim Champy, business consultant and coauthor of *Reengineering the Corporation*

"Great popular musicians must simultaneously master tight structures and freeform improvisation, selfless collaboration, and solitary self-expression, artistry, and commerce. What a treat to get an inside look at the creative process and enterprising spirit of some of the most talented people on the planet."

—Scott Dadich, creator of *Abstract: The Art of Design*, recipient of the National Design Award, and former editor in chief of *WIRED*

"Being an artist isn't just a matter of having imaginative ideas—to make songs and put them out into the world, you have to use that imagination to problem-solve, collaborate, pivot, and hustle. This book shows how thinking like a musician can provide valuable lessons for entrepreneurs, educators, and anyone who's trying to create something new."

—Hrishikesh Hirway, creator and host of *Song Exploder*

"We all know that creativity plays a major role in the world of music, and that innovation plays a major role in the world of business. But are creativity and innovation two sides of a coin? Like the subjects it writes about, *Two Beats Ahead* is a highly creative, innovative, and enjoyable book."

—Irving Wladawsky-Berger, former chairman, Board of Governors, IBM Academy of Technology, and research affiliate, MIT Sloan School of Management

two
beats
ahead

two beats ahead

What Musical Minds Teach Us About Innovation

Panos A. Panay and R. Michael Hendrix

PUBLICAFFAIRS

New York

PublicAffairs
Hachette Book Group
1290 Avenue of the Americas, New York, NY 10104
www.publicaffairsbooks.com
@Public_Affairs

Printed in the United States of America

First Edition: April 2021

Published by PublicAffairs, an imprint of Perseus Books, LLC, a subsidiary of Hachette Book Group, Inc. The PublicAffairs name and logo is a trademark of the Hachette Book Group.

The Hachette Speakers Bureau provides a wide range of authors for speaking events. To find out more, go to www.hachettespeakersbureau.com or call (866) 376-6591.

The publisher is not responsible for websites (or their content) that are not owned by the publisher.

Print book interior design by Amy Quinn

Library of Congress Cataloging-in-Publication Data
Names: Panay, Panos A., author. | Hendrix, R. Michael, author.
Title: Two beats ahead : what musical minds teach us about innovation / Panos A. Panay and R. Michael Hendrix.
Description: First edition. | New York : PublicAffairs, 2021. | Includes bibliographical references and index.
Identifiers: LCCN 2020029610 | ISBN 9781541730588 (hardcover) | ISBN 9781541730571 (ebook)
Subjects: LCSH: Musicians—Psychology. | Creative ability in business. | Entrepreneurship. | Creation (Literary, artistic, etc.)
Classification: LCC ML3838 .P29 2021 | DDC 338.4/778—dc23
LC record available at https://lccn.loc.gov/2020029610

ISBNs: 978-1-5417-3058-8 (hardcover); 978-1-5417-0049-9 (international); 978-1-5417-3057-1 (ebook)

LSC-C

Printing 1, 2021

contents

prelude

Music is the skeleton key that opens every door.

—Pharrell Williams

In Boston's Back Bay neighborhood, just blocks from Fenway Park and the Charles River, sits a twelve-hundred seat performance hall on the campus of Berklee College of Music. On an unseasonably cold April day in 2018, every seat was filled with students, faculty, and guests, with eyes fixed on a large screen suspended over the stage.

When the screen blinked to life, it was filled by the larger-than-life grin of Pharrell Williams. He had beamed in by Skype from his home in California to talk to the Berklee community about the artist as start-up. Pharrell is a musician and producer who has won eleven Grammy Awards and an Oscar nomination for his work with collaborators, including Daft Punk, Jay-Z, Justin

1

Timberlake, and Robin Thicke. He is equally well known for his work as a design director, creating sneakers for Adidas, Chanel, Reebok, and Timberland; eyewear and jewelry for Louis Vuitton; down jackets for Moncler; and a fragrance for Comme des Garçons.

But before the conversation started, Panos thanked Pharrell for joining, especially since it was on his birthday. At that, a group of five students stood up from their seats and began singing "Happy Birthday to You" a cappella, then seamlessly shifted, after a few bars, into a sunny, stomping rendition of Pharrell's hit song "Happy."

When the music stopped, Pharrell bowed graciously to the singers in thanks, and then began the conversation with a simple statement: "Music is the skeleton key that opens every door." He went on to say that mindsets he had learned in the recording studio—following his intuition, collaborating with others, trusting his own voice, and exploring new outlets for expression—had also led to success in his many business ventures.

"I'm always curious about new sounds, new textures, new ways of expressing myself," he told us. "I think curiosity is where it begins for me. There are people who focus on one thing singularly, and that works for them. But a lot of us, including people here in the audience today, need to be able to express ourselves in different ways. When we do, we enjoy the fruits of having seeds in many different grounds."

For nearly three decades, Pharrell has applied these mindsets to both art and business. As a musician, whether in live performance or in the studio, he is adept at trading in emotion, building upon the logic of chords and scales to connect with audiences. These same tools have equipped him as a creative director for global brands and fashion houses and to connect with customers. In many ways, he is the embodiment of the ideas that we will explore in the pages following: that the mindsets developed by musicians make them good entrepreneurs. That artists, executives, and creative spirits can draw upon these skills—whether as small business owners, visionaries looking to get a start-up off the ground, nonprofit managers, or leaders in the gig economy.

And, of course, it's not just Pharrell. While working on this book, we sat down with Justin Timberlake to talk about songwriting, Imogen Heap about experimentation, Hank Shocklee and T Bone Burnett about shaping environments for creative expression, Prince's sound engineer Susan Rogers about prototyping, Madame Gandhi about connecting with audiences, Jimmy Iovine about listening for gaps in the market, and many others. We also talked with leaders from Google X and Amazon.

We realize that these are conversations that don't happen every day. In our professional lives—Panos as senior vice president for global strategy and innovation at Berklee, and Michael as global design director at IDEO—we're lucky that doors are open to us as musicians, as veteran founders of successful start-ups, and now as executives of organizations that are globally acclaimed for innovation. But neither of us began our career the way businesspeople are "supposed to"; we have no pedigrees from Ivy League business schools or internships with disruption gurus.

Yet even before we met, we independently realized that our backgrounds in music are key to our success. That the creative mindset is more than a unique approach to entrepreneurship, more than drawing upon the improvisation of jazz or practicing until our fingers bleed. Since we started sharing thoughts with each other, we've only been confirmed in our belief that music cultivates an essential way of thinking and working in business—especially in today's deconstructed, discombobulated, and unpredictable world.

When we sit and talk together, we laugh a lot. We swap old band stories as easily as we talk about unlocking the creative genius of kids in Abu Dhabi or Shanghai. And as we have taught, traveled, and consulted with clients, we've been delighted to discover that there are many like-minded people who feel, perhaps without knowing the words for this feeling, that this idea has merit.

So we think of this book as a conversation between the two of us, the amazing artists and entrepreneurs we've been lucky to interview, and you as a reader. In other words, be forewarned: this isn't a how-to manual. It's not a "Seven Easy Steps to Success" seminar. It's not a drawn-out blog post of fifty-four things to try today. Rather, it's an ongoing dialogue that we hope will inspire you to think about your business, your goals, pretty much everything, through the lens of the musical mindset. You'll read about creativity and collaboration, listening and openness, and trust and fear and how all of this relates to working in today's marketplace. But above all, you'll see how the musical mindset can be a new framework of seeing and responding to a dynamic world, a constant learning and growth approach that mirrors the openness and adaptability of music making but applied onto a whole new context. The mindsets we discuss in the pages following are not only helpful, they are necessary—and they are lacking. Our schools prioritize coding classes over art; our workplaces reward algorithms and analytical thinking. Artificial intelligence and big data are the pursuit du jour in corporate playbooks. Although we recognize the value of all of the above, we also see a real gap, an urgent need, for the kind of imaginative thinking needed now to tackle our society's increasingly complex challenges. It's not about making the false choice between science *or* art, mathematics *or* music, but about emphasizing both. After all, it's no coincidence that arguably humanity's greatest mind, Leonardo da Vinci, was both scientist *and* artist and seamlessly used one discipline to inform the other. Artists and entrepreneurs alike work and produce better work when they learn to listen, experiment, collaborate, demo, produce, connect, remix, sense, and constantly reinvent. Our world is no longer defined by brick and mortar. The possibilities are endless.

One more thing: as you read each chapter, we encourage you to sit with the insights, anecdotes, and information, letting them sink in. So at the end of each chapter we've created an interlude, a playlist of songs by the artists you've just read about that can easily be found on your favorite streaming service. Give the songs a listen, not only to get to know the artists better but also to give your mind a breather, a bit of space to process what you just read. You'll find, as we have in conversation after conversation, that great ideas from amazing artists take on new shapes, mixing with your own thoughts—and who knows what they'll spark? But the first step is critical, and, in our experience, it all starts with listening.

one
listening

The Space Between the Notes

*The most powerful thing is often the thing
which lies slumbering in the silence.*

—Björk

Imagine . . .

... standing in an audience of ten thousand people at Red Rocks Amphitheater, a geologically formed, open-air venue in the mountains west of Denver. On each side of the stadium seats are three-hundred-foot-tall, 200-million-year-old sandstone monoliths that have shaped acoustic perfection for bands like the Beatles, Jimi Hendrix, Bruce Springsteen, and U2. It's a late summer night in 2018, and you're on your feet, along with everyone else in the crowd, at Illenium's sold-out show.

Illenium is an electronic dance music (EDM) artist and DJ who mixes his live performances in real time, backed by a band that includes a piano, guitars, and five drum kits. The stage set is a spectacle by design: the musicians play framed against gigantic screens that flash video clips as you dance among the other shadowed figures in the strobing lights. Now and then, bursts of pyrotechnics light the upturned faces around you. But halfway through the hit song "Silence," Illenium's collaboration with megasinger Khalid, the screen goes dark and twin spotlights shine on a lone guitarist repeating four bars of a simple melody over and over again. Behind him, the band dials back, foregrounding Khalid's gentle, fluid vocals. This goes on for more than a minute before all five drummers make their way back into the song, picking up the thread, beating a rhythm that sounds almost like a military march, increasing in intensity and speed. Everyone around you stops dancing: it's hard to find a beat to follow, to know how to move, as the energy shifts from kinetic to potential, building tension, building anticipation.

Then, precisely at two minutes and twenty-two seconds into the song, the music stops.

It's only a pause, not even for a full second, but it creates overwhelming drama. And when the song starts again it is with a massive bass drop, every instrument on stage at full volume. You can feel it in your chest, like the downhill fall on a high-flying roller coaster, an incredible release that floods the amphitheater, bouncing off the cliff walls and out into the desert night.

Creating a moment of silence before "dropping the beat" is a popular technique in the clubs and concert venues where EDM reigns, but it has a much longer history. In the late 1700s, classical composer Josef Haydn often wrote pauses into his compositions to build tension with audiences. His string quartet from Opus 33, nicknamed "The Joke," calls for a cellist and three violinists to stop midpiece. Not just to pause, but to stop playing completely; in some performances, the musicians go so far as to put down their instruments. When the audience begins to applaud, the performers start again: the song isn't over yet. The crowd sits back in their seats. When the notes fade away a second time, the audience claps again, but the musicians cut them short once more, picking up where they left off. The third and final time, the audience is awkward, unsure of what to do. Silence fills the performance hall, displacing sound with curiosity.

An even more famously provocative use of silence in music is John Cage's "4'33"." Written in the late 1940s, Cage's composition instructs a musician to walk onstage, bow, pull out the bench at a piano, and sit. And sit. And sit. For four minutes and thirty-three seconds, everyone waits but not a single key is struck. Audience members who have never seen the piece performed before squirm in their chairs for a few minutes, but gradually everyone becomes keenly aware of the ambient sounds in the room. The rustle of a program. A cough from the balcony. The clacking heels of someone walking through the lobby. A car passing in the street outside. All sounds that were present all along, yet unnoticed. At the end of four minutes and thirty-three seconds, the pianist stands, bows once more, and leaves the stage.

In his book *Silence*, Cage insists that music both requires and includes the absence of music. "Formerly silence was the time lapse between sounds, useful toward a variety of ends, among them that of tasteful arrangement," he writes. "Where none of these goals is present, silence becomes something else—not silence at all, but sounds, the ambient sounds."

Of course, these are deliberately provocative examples. But think for a moment: every song you have ever heard makes use of the space between notes. This space is what gives a song its rhythm and texture; what is not played is as important as what is. We might miss the rests, stops, and intervals because we have been conditioned to expect what is familiar—that is, until someone breaks the pattern and grabs our attention.

How did you react when you came across the eight blank pages at the beginning of this chapter? Maybe you flipped forward, looking for the words you expected. After all, we've been conditioned since childhood: turning a page means that the story continues. But did you notice anything in yourself as you found blank page after blank page? Maybe thoughts flashed through your head like: "Why is this going on for so long?" or "Oh boy, I bet someone at the printer got fired!"

Why should a book not have blank pages if it's for a purpose? The vast majority of songs on the radio are designed to deliver exactly what we expect: a great intro, a hummable hook, a repeated chorus. But music can also confound assumptions and release you from the trap of expectations so that you discover something new and beautiful.

As musicians, we believe that there is something instructive here for our work as entrepreneurs and business leaders. Musicians know how to create moments that break patterns, fill gaps, capture our attention, and inspire not only because of skills they have developed at a keyboard or a microphone, but because they have honed their ability to listen.

Like any musical skill, listening takes practice. The beginner student has to count keys on a piano to find the right note, while a professional can sit blindfolded and play by feel. In this chapter, we're going to explore examples of musicians and entrepreneurs who have learned to listen to the world around them, as well as to their own internal sense of what works. Both involve being present and open to the unexpected. Whether you are channeling your creativity, building a dynamic company, or leading a team, a musical mindset can play a key role—if you know how to look for the space between the notes.

Listening for the Gaps

From 1990 to 2006, Jimmy Iovine was best known as a founder of Interscope Records, the record label representing an incredible variety of bands, from the Black Eyed Peas to Eminem, Limp Bizkit, Marilyn Manson, and U2. But in the midaughts, Jimmy saw that the industry was rapidly evolving. A nineteen-year-old computer hacker named Shawn Fanning and a budding entrepreneur named Sean Parker had created Napster, a platform for anyone to share music, for free, with anyone else using the software. Music could be downloaded for free and nearly instantaneously. We sat down with Jimmy to talk about this shift and how it led him to an idea that changed not only his life but how we all listen to music.

"In the early 2000s, Napster came out and my first thought was: I get that. This is a problem for the labels. Clearly, the record industry needed to learn a few more tricks."

With changes coming fast, Jimmy started looking for new ways to generate revenue. He explored a collaboration with Diesel, the Italian clothing company. He dug into streaming options. But it was in a collaboration with his longtime friend, hip-hop pioneer, and superproducer Dr. Dre, that he found his $3 billion idea.

"What was clear was that we needed to get into business with artists," he said. "We needed to have a relationship with our customers. We have to do other things that are part of popular culture. Dre would complain to me that his kids were listening to his music on computers and with cheap earbuds. He hated that because he had spent hundreds of hours on every sound. And the little white Apple earbuds that were everywhere? Even Steve Jobs said that they were never meant to be the standard for listening to music; they were just starter buds to test out the iPhone."

One day, Jimmy ran into Dre on the beach. Dre was frustrated, sharing with Jimmy that he was tired of brands asking him to endorse their products, to use his name to drive sales. This was nothing new: for years, he had been asked to partner with various brands, particularly sneaker companies, but he had always said no because he had no personal connection to the product. Jimmy said that he immediately told Dre: you should do speakers not sneakers. Headphones. What if they could make the experience of listening to music as cool as the music itself?

At the time, this might have seemed like a bit of an odd choice. To most people, headphones were a commodity. The shelves at Walmart were crowded with inexpensive options, and companies that sold phones or MP3 players gave them away for free. But Jimmy intuitively felt that an intimate, authentic, real, and direct connection could be created between an artist and an audience at the moment that the artist's music touched the listener's ears, and that most headphones were selling that experience short.

"If we could create something that captured an artist's intent, their vision, on kids' heads, they would feel something different than they felt through those earplugs," he told us. "They wouldn't know what hit them because they've never actually had great headphones before."

Iovine and Dre started by inviting a team from Bose Corporation to Interscope to meet about a collaboration. At the time, Bose was the undisputed industry heavyweight for audiophiles who were willing to spend thousands of dollars on noise-canceling headphones, state-of-the-art sound systems, and accessories. But when the Bose engineers visited Interscope, it quickly became apparent that they had never been in a recording studio. Bose subscribed to a methodology of designing and fine-tuning sound systems on computers, according to the laws of physics and mathematics, using classical compositions as a sound reference. Their headphones were amazing at canceling out background noise and giving high-quality sound. But they fell short when it came to listening to popular music, with its distinct layers of sound and pumping beats.

Buckle up, we're about to get a bit nerdy. Headphones are designed and engineered with a sound stage in mind—a technical term for virtual proximity to the source. Think of the last time you were at a concert, standing in the middle of the crowd, fifty feet or more from the stage. What did it sound like? Not only do you hear the band, you also hear the people around you, the space between your ears, and the microphones. Now think of a time when you made your way closer to the stage, just a few feet away from the singer. The difference in what you hear is called the sound stage. Modern recording technologies make it possible for listeners to have a much more intimate proximity to the sources of sound. Rather than listening to the blended sounds of a room, you can be standing onstage with the band.

For Iovine and Dre, the aural intent of pop artists was missing from most headphone experiences—as was the heavy bass beat that characterizes so much of today's music. Drawing upon long careers in studios, Iovine and Dre wanted to create headphones with a sound stage that honored how artists want their music to be heard. Mathematical principles of sound are, of course, important, as are market analytics like demographics, retail penetration, and price comparison, but human experience is front and center. At the end of the day, when we tune into our favorite songs, we are not looking for a Platonic ideal of sound quality—we want to hear the music as the artist intended. And who better to know this than producers who have spent thousands of hours in the studio, helping artists create their unique sound?

Paul Wachter, financial adviser to investors, including Iovine, LeBron James, and Bono, was involved in the formation of Dr. Dre and Jimmy Iovine's headphones, eventually called Beats. When we sat down with him, Paul talked about watching Iovine and Beats test out prototypes for their headphones.

"When they were testing prototypes," Paul said, "they each listened to the same song over and over again, through every pair of headphones. For Jimmy, it was a song he had personally produced for Tom Petty. Dre always listened to 50 Cent's 'In Da Club,' which he had produced. They listened to every prototype, every version, using the same two songs, because they knew exactly what each song was supposed to sound like since they had produced those songs, they had engineered those songs, had heard them in the studio, had discussed them with the artists."

When we asked Jimmy about this, he chuckled. "That's true. I know what Tom Petty's record is supposed to sound like because I made it. I mixed it, I mastered it. More importantly, I knew what it was supposed to feel like. The biggest complaint we got about the original version of Beats was that they weren't audiophile grade: they weren't precision engineered in a lab for sound quality. But that wasn't the point. I remember bringing Trent Reznor of Nine Inch Nails and the guy who produces Smashing Pumpkins to Interscope to try out the original Beats. These are bands with big sound, and when their heads started nodding, we knew we were onto something. What we were after was the soul and feel of recording in a studio. Turns out that listeners, like artists, don't give a shit about audiophile grade; they want their shit to sound good."

Jimmy and Dre's first headphones, Beats by Dre, debuted in 2008. They were an unprecedented marriage of technology and culture, with the bass-heavy experience and fashion sensibility that people craved. Within months, Jimmy gave a pair of headphones to LeBron James, who went on to give a pair to each of his teammates on the 2008 Olympics US basketball team. It was a marketing coup: the most famous basketball team in the country got off the plane in Beijing, all wearing a new brand of headphones—one that tapped not only a new sound experience but also the culture of music. British tennis player Laura Robson tweeted about receiving a pair of Beats with a Union Jack design. None of the athletes were paid to wear or endorse Beats; they didn't have to be. The momentum carried the product forward.

Six years later, Apple acquired Beats for $2.6 billion. In the years since, the sound quality has improved even further and even influenced the engineering behind Apple's AirPods. As we listened to Jimmy recount some of these stories, it was apparent that his ability not only to listen for trends and gaps in the market but also to attach sound to culture and artists' intent to audiences—feeling to listening—were at play.

"One of the engineers at Apple once asked me what I mean by feel. It's everything, everything in your life. When you look at a painting, you feel something. You might walk through a gallery and see ten paintings, but only one of them hits you. It's the same when you hear a great song: you feel something and interpret it inside your head. When it feels right, it feels right."

"The thing to remember," he told us, "is that I didn't know Beats was going to work. We had a great idea and understood the basis for its potential. Kids were listening to music on headphones that sounded terrible and that looked like medical equipment. We were interested in the power of music, the power of culture. Marry these two things together, then make it sexy, and we can jump over gatekeepers to build demand. We did an ad with Nets forward Kevin Garnett, and one of the marketing guys said: we should get someone bigger, more famous. But I said no, Kevin is known for his intensity, for his authenticity. Kevin is Beats; his attitude is what the Beats attitude should be. So he is walking into a rival stadium, and people are cursing at him and throwing things, but he puts on his Beats and says: hear what you want. When that kind of thing happens, that's going to win."

With a $3 billion buyout, it might sound like Iovine and Dre won the lottery, but the true value of their brand came from their insistence upon the importance of the musical experience—rooted in listening to what both musicians and fans want. It's important to note that they didn't conduct surveys or polls; instead, they paid attention to the silence, the absence, the gaps. Their story reminds us of advice the jazz trumpet master Miles Davis often told his collaborators: "Don't play what's there. Play what's not there." As educators and innovators, we see the value of this impulse time and time again. It is possible for us to hone our hunches and learn to feel for what's in the gaps.

Finding the Starting Point

Desmond Child is a Songwriters Hall of Fame inductee who has written more than two thousand songs. His hits include Bon Jovi's "Living on a Prayer" and "You Give Love a Bad Name," Ricky Martin's "La Vida Loca," Barbra Streisand's "Lady Liberty," and "Thong Song" by Sisqó. Other collaborators include Aerosmith, Cher, Katy Perry, Kelly Clarkson, Kiss, and Michael Bolton. How has Desmond managed to be so prolific and work successfully with so many artists, spanning genres and generations?

When we first met him, we wondered if Desmond would be imposing and intimidating, a man who is aware of his fame and influence, a celebrity's celebrity. We were delighted to discover that he is a warm and engaging person, the kind of friend you could talk to forever. To give a quick example of the kind of person he is: during our first conversation with him, Panos mentioned in passing that he was born and grew up in Cyprus. So imagine our surprise when, months later, Panos was invited to Desmond's home in New York and was introduced to another Cypriot couple, as well as a Cyprus-born chef whom Desmond had asked to cook a traditional meal of *halloumi* cheese, *horiatiki* salad, and grilled *lavraki*. It was more than a thoughtful gesture; it was typical Desmond.

That evening's meal stretched out for hours. After dinner, we talked about how he learned to write hit songs. He said that his musical education started in infancy, when he lay in a crib next to his mother—the late, great Cuban bolero writer Elena Casals—while she played the piano.

"She was a poet," he told us. "When she was happy, she'd write a happy song; when she was sad, she'd write a sad song. Her music was a snapshot of her daily life."

His mother's translation of slices of life, small moments of delight or sadness, into music and lyrics inspired Desmond to form Desmond Child & Rouge, a rhythm-and-blues-influenced pop band, in the mid-1970s. The band received positive reviews, and its music was included on a movie soundtrack. One of the band's songs climbed to number fifty-one on the Billboard charts but sold poorly. So Desmond looked to transition into songwriting, and connected with Bob Crewe, the legendary songwriter for the Four Seasons, Bobby Darin, Patti LaBelle, and Barry Manilow.

"For two years, Bob and I would get together at a little place for lunch, across the street from his studio," he said. "Monday through Friday I'd meet him at noon, and he'd tell me stories about the old days in Hollywood. Then we'd go to his studio—a bare apartment with nothing on the walls, nothing in it but a grand piano and a chair for him to sit in."

Desmond describes sitting at the piano in the spare room with Crewe in the chair beside him, both with blank pads of paper. According to Crewe's method, they were searching not for a melody or lyric but for a song's title.

"Bob would not begin writing a song until he had a great title. I would throw out an idea and then he would until—bingo!—we nailed it. Bob felt that the title should encapsulate the whole essence and story of a song in a few words and that writing the lyrics should be about finding their way back to this essence."

In Desmond's mind, Crewe's technique dovetailed with that of his mother: listen for the right way into a song, patiently working until you can sum up a human experience in a few words and a turn of phrase. Taken together, these ideas changed Desmond's life when he had the opportunity to collaborate with New Jersey rocker Jon Bon Jovi. Desmond was invited to the childhood home of Bon Jovi's guitarist Richie Sambora, a small wooden house on

the edge of a brown marsh with an oil refinery in the distance—
an archetypal childhood setting for a member of an archetypal
Americana band. Bon Jovi, Sambora, and Desmond met in the
basement, where Sambora had set up a keyboard and a shabby,
buzzing amplifier on a Formica table.

"Thinking back to my sessions with Bob, I had already thought
of a title and brought it in my back pocket: 'You Give Love a Bad
Name.' The minute I said it, Jon's face lit up, and I got my first view
of that billion-dollar smile. Turns out he had also been working on
a song, and he threw out, 'Shot through the heart and you're to
blame because darling . . .'

"Then the three of us chimed in: 'You give love a bad name.'"

What rejected teenage Romeo or Juliet hasn't felt this pain? It
was as if Desmond could hear their unspoken sighs and channeled
them into pop poetry and then turned them into a creative relationship that lasted for many years. "You Give Love a Bad Name"
reached number one on the Billboard Hot 100, became a number-
one hit again in Poland when the singer Mandaryna recorded it,
and had yet another stint on the charts when a contestant performed it on *American Idol*.

Listening to Yourself

Desmond's practice of drawing on personal experience and dis-
tilling it into a few words is only one starting point for creativity.
For many songwriters and creatives, as well as entrepreneurs, the
question of where to begin can seem daunting. There is something
intimidating about a blank page; you have ideas rolling around in
your head, like socks tumbling in a dryer, but don't quite know
how to reach in and pull out the right one, the one with a thread
that you can follow. Desmond starts by listening for the perfect
title. Others look for intense emotional experiences and try to
catch their feeling and then catapult it into audiences. For Icelandic
singer and composer Björk, her process begins with immersing
herself in nature.

A native of Reykjavik, Iceland, Björk is deeply committed to the idea of listening to the natural world around her and interpreting what she hears into art. Like Desmond, she started young. Even as a child, walking in the woods or singing for her classmates on the school bus, she said that singing is her way of interacting with her environment. And the interaction is not abstract; it's particular. She has spoken in interviews about walking along the pier in Reykjavik, listening to the noises of the harbor: waves lapping on the shore, the cries of seagulls overhead, the horns of ships in traffic. To Björk, this is more than background noise; it is music. Her song "Wanderlust" begins with these sounds, seemingly at random until they come together and harmonize, falling into a rhythm that becomes the backbone of the melody. From the mundane soundtrack of everyday life, Björk took what she heard—or, more accurately, listened to closely—and orchestrated a lovely and haunting song about what it means to belong.

As she has grown to become the most famous Icelandic artist of all time, she has released a catalog of songs that are unorthodox, otherworldly, idiosyncratic, and beautiful—and that have become international hits. She describes her process of artistic creation, whether in music, fashion, music videos, or starring in movies like Lars von Trier's *Dancer in the Dark*, as a search for emotional coordinates.

"I started writing melodies as a kid, walking to school and back, and it just always was my way of coping or dealing with the world," Björk has said. "It's like another function in my subconscious, in my brain that's just rolling away like a screensaver, coexisting next to whatever is happening . . . if there is a happy period or if there's a sad period, or I have all the time in the world or no time in the world, it's just something that's kind of bubbling underneath."

Over time, Björk has honed her habit of listening to a reflex. She makes it sound easy. But just like learning to play an instrument takes years of practice, it takes years to make the skill of listening effortless. Her antennae are always up, like a satellite dish catching waves from distant galaxies, separating the signal from the noise. Appearing on an episode of the podcast *Song Exploder*, she reveals how she dials in the signal, describing the process of sonically exploring emotions, with another of her hits, "Stonemilker."

"I was walking on a beach back and forth and the lyrics came along without me editing them [and I thought] moments of clarity are so rare, I'd better document this," she said. "The strength of this album is simplicity, thinking out loud, feeling, and I shouldn't be too clever. It would work against it. The whole song is about wanting clarity, wanting simplicity, and talking to someone who wants things to be really complex and foggy and unclear. And you saying: 'OK, I've got clarity, want it or not.'"

It takes practice and, perhaps just as importantly, a deliberate decision to recognize what is not there or at least what is not normally there. In this case, it was a lucid moment that matches the intent of her song. That was the signal.

In "The Songwriters Issue" of *Q* magazine, published in 2007, she further unpacked her process of identifying, exploring, and articulating emotional connections.

"It's all about singing the melodies live in my head. They go in circles. I guess I'm quite conservative and romantic about the power of melodies. I try not to record them on my Dictaphone when I first hear them. If I forget all about it and it pops up later on, then I know it's good enough. I let my subconscious do the editing."

When the time comes to add lyrics, she says:

"I put a lot of work into the lyrics, and I think there is a reason why the written word and the poetic form allow us to express things we can't express during our everyday lives or in conversation," she said. "These few times you manage to arrange the words in the correct order you create this tension and this energy, which flows between the lines, and the most powerful thing is often the thing which lies slumbering in the silence."

At this point, you might be wondering what an Icelandic post-punk sprite's search for emotional connections in the world around her has to do with entrepreneurship. Unless you're planning to write an esoteric, existential, international number-one hit, how does this relate to the world of business?

But stay with us. A musician understands that listening to the world, drawing ideas and inspiration from outside yourself, is only the first part of innovation. It also requires listening to yourself for points of resonance between the world and your own vision and values. And in Björk's case, the power of her approach took on new meaning when she helped her country through a crippling economic recession.

Listening to Yourself

The global financial crisis of 2008 started in Iceland. In a country of three hundred thousand people, there were only three private banks, each of which had grown fat in the years leading up to the crisis, thanks to governmental policies that encouraged them to borrow heavily. A new moneyed elite sprang up in the country, thanks to easy access to large lines of credit: the housing market ballooned and stock market prices increased by 900 percent in a single year. Over the course of three years, the average Icelander's personal wealth grew by 300 percent. But when the bubble burst, all three banks defaulted, investment firms went belly up, and more than a quarter of Icelanders couldn't pay their mortgages.

Björk felt a responsibility to do what she could to take care of her fellow citizens, so she teamed up with a venture capital company called Audur Capital. Audur's founders, Halla Tomasdottir and Kristin Petursdottir, had earned a reputation for investing in environmentally sustainable projects and female entrepreneurs, but with Audur's BJÖRK venture fund they went a step further.

Following the singer's lead, they listened for emotional connections that aligned with their own values. When considering potential investments for the fund, Audur's founders said that their
personal feelings about a company were just as important as historical data, market gap analysis, and projections.

"We were willing to use our rational mind *and* our emotional
intelligence to release value out of our investments," they told the
BBC in 2009. "The touchy-feely side is actually the harder side.
We reject a lot more investment opportunities as a result of emotional due diligence than financial due diligence."

Let's pause for a moment to consider whether or not *emotional
due diligence* is a term you have heard before. We certainly had
not—and it made us stop and consider: Why is that? After all,
people invest in people; a company's leaders shape its vision, culture, and ability to deliver.

We called venture capitalist Tim Chang to ask for his thoughts
about this concept of emotional due diligence. Tim started his
career as a musician: he grew up playing classical piano, but in
high school he joined a rock band, and from the day he played Van
Halen's "Eruption" on stage, he felt less like a bookish teen and
more like a rock star. His fellow classmates suddenly were not just
friends, they were fans. Following the feeling, Tim pursued music
throughout college, signed a record deal with Sony, and started
touring.

But he soon realized that the contracts offered by Sony did not
line up with his personal values—the label profited, while the musicians sweated—and so he left the road to enter the world of finance. Now a partner with Silicon Valley titan Mayfield, Tim has
twice been named to the Forbes Midas List of top tech investors.
His personal journey from tour bus to tech stardom involved an
honest rethink of who he is and what he wants to spend his time
and effort building.

"As a musician, when I started playing in bands, I had to unlearn a lot of my classical training and really figure out: What

is my voice? What am I trying to say? What's my style? I went through a lot of different genres, picking up the elements that resonated with me. I call it creating my own mixtape. I think that's the number-one job of an artist: craft your own voice."

He followed a similar path when he shifted into finance.

"When I started, I tried to come up with a formula for whether or not to invest in a company. I wanted a heuristic, a scoring criteria, so I started by looking at hundreds and hundreds of examples, getting data points down and looking for patterns."

Despite Tim's rigorous analysis, he, too, came to lean heavily on emotional due diligence. When an entrepreneur presents to Mayfield, a great idea is enough to get you in the door but not close a deal. Tim also looks at historic data: the individual's past track of personal or professional achievement, for signs of chutzpah, initiative, and self-awareness.

"What the X factors are for me might not be the X factors for someone else," he told us. "Maybe you are drawn to rule breakers. Maybe you are not. But it's important to know what matters to you personally. It will vary wildly from person to person, just like who I fall in love with is different from who you fall in love with. It's as much an art of understanding yourself as it is understanding others."

Given his own radical pursuit of self-awareness, it's no surprise that he listens for the same in others. There is a common perception that, when pitching an idea to a roomful of investor millionaires, an entrepreneur should have everything buttoned up, can't let her guard down, can't show weaknesses in the plan. For Tim, this is a yellow flag. So much so that he often asks pitchers to talk about the most difficult challenges they have faced in their careers or even outside the workplace.

"Their response tells me so much. If they are defensive, or if they're open and vulnerable, or if they have no clue what you're talking about, that's really revealing. I want to invest in people who have done the work."

In his emotional due diligence, Tim is looking for people with whom he is on the same wavelength. He chuckled as he told us that he sometimes imagines a small, energy-producing motor inside everyone, vibrating at different frequencies.

"Each person emanates that energy subtly, all the time, and as you get more attuned to your own self and your own energy, you get better at reading other people's and, even better, building connections."

For Björk, Audur Capital, and Tim Chang, building an investment portfolio is grounded on a different kind of thinking, one based in feeling. They listen to their gut intuition as a reliable guide. The same goes for Pharrell Williams, though he took the idea of listening to and trusting your own voice ever further:

"Everybody has some level of doubt, somewhere. But for the most part, there's a healthy portion of delusion that is required for us to be artists. You have to believe that you are worthy and have to believe that you are unique and have something different. You can doubt, but doubting is a nonstarter. You can't get anything started that way. I was just with an artist the other day who continued to talk himself out of something that was really amazing, and it was blowing my mind. That is what you don't want. You *want* a healthy delusion."

Escaping Ego

At this point in our narrative, you might assume we're claiming that artists and entrepreneurs should trust their ability to see opportunities and act on them in ways that align with their vision—in other words, that it's possible to be infallible. But we're all wrong sometimes. How do you know when you should change direction? Again: the key is to stay open and keep listening.

The concept of a pivot is as familiar to entrepreneurs as the bass drop is to EDM musicians. Composer and social entrepreneur Mike Cassidy is no stranger to the concept. A graduate of both Berklee College of Music and Harvard Business School, Cassidy cofounded four internet companies before becoming director of product management at Google, where he led Google X's Project Loon, which uses enormous hot air balloons flown at an altitude of sixty thousand feet to bring LTE wireless to disaster zones, underserved populations, and other areas where internet connectivity is not available. Never one to settle, he raised the stakes again, leaving Google and founding a nuclear energy start-up called Apollo Fusion.

"In four out of my first five start-ups," he told us, "our first idea failed, and we had to change direction. When I was in my early twenties, I realized that I was spending a lot of time rethinking decisions after I made them. Should I go back and change my mind? At one point I calculated that I was spending half of my thought cycles rehashing decisions I had already made. So I made a resolution never to rethink a decision once I had made it."

He enforces this in his start-ups, too. The team looks at all available data, hashes out a plan, and then agrees to focus all of their energy on making it work. But after an agreed-upon time, they look at the data again. If things are not going in the right direction, they make changes.

In 1994, Mike's company Dial-a-Fish set out to change how the world shops for groceries in the days before internet shopping. Along the way, the team realized that the computer telephony tools on the market were not meeting their needs, so they built the tool that they wished they could find. As it turns out, other companies needed a similar tool, so Mike pivoted the company to focus on building the first Microsoft-based telephony application, rebranding as Stylus Innovation. Within six months, they were the market leader and two years later sold the company for $13 million, ten thousand times the founders' investment.

This same approach proved useful when he started Ultimate Arena, a platform where users could win real money by playing video games online. The idea tanked, and so Mike's team asked their customers why they stopped using it. Many replied that they only signed up because the platform made it easy to play online with their friends, on a shared server. The company retooled as Xfire, an instant messenger app for gamers, which sold to Viacom in 2006 for $102 million.

In entrepreneur lore, it's easy to forget that stories like Mike's are out of the ordinary. We can all imagine ourselves as the next Zuckerberg or Cassidy, recasting failures as a "pivot," nothing more than a stepping-stone on the road to success. But Mike was candid with us about just how deeply challenging and humbling the experience can be. Investors who signed up to back one business now have to get excited about a different idea; the same is true of team members. However, it can work if a pivot is grounded in listening for opportunities and finding new alignments.

Implicit in our conversations with both Tim and Mike is an important lesson: it's essential to get ego out of the way. Open yourself up, be aware and watchful, be listening.

We saw this idea in action when we brought together a group of tech CEOs at Boston's Café ArtScience in May of 2017 with a shared objective of talking about the intersection between music and entrepreneurship. The event's organizer, Silicon Valley Bank, regularly hosts events to encourage leadership development within its portfolio companies. When they asked us to share our thoughts on musical mindsets and entrepreneurial behaviors, we saw it as a perfect opportunity to test our theory about the mindset of listening with an audience of young start-up founders.

When our guests arrived, they walked into a room with couches and chairs arranged in a loose circle. In the center was an upright bass, a snare drum, and a saxophone. The evening started with a presentation similar to many of our initial class lectures: a look at the disruptive forces in the music industry and a celebration of the resilient musicians who have navigated it, from Skrillex to Bowie, and how an artist's mindset of productivity enables him to continuously adapt to the changes happening around him.

Half an hour into the event, Panos invited three people to the center of the room. Up until this point, they had been standing quietly
at the back, on the periphery: three young men wearing dress jackets and ties. They were music students from local universities who
had never met before. Something new was about to happen.

Panos set up the experience by saying, let's not overexplain the
value of a musical mindset when it comes to listening; instead, let's
witness it. After a brief conversation, the three students eased their
way into a jazz standard, "Autumn Leaves," composed by Joseph
Kosma and Jacques Prévert, with an English language version
written by Johnny Mercer. In 1955, an instrumental version by pianist Roger Williams hit number one on the US Billboard charts.
Within minutes, the students were playing together as if they had
been rehearsing the song for weeks. No one could tell that they
had never met before that evening.

But still: these were musicians, trained in foundational skills,
tuned to listen and collaborate with each other. So Panos invited one of the executives in attendance to come to a keyboard
set up at the front of the room. Janet Comenos is CEO of Spot-
ted Media, a data company that helps brands and agencies make
smarter celebrity-based marketing decisions; she is also a singer-
songwriter. At Panos's request, she began playing an original song
that none of the musicians had heard before.

What happened next was astounding. At first, Janet was a
bit hesitant, but one of the students told her: "It's OK, just play
through your mistakes. We'll join along." And as Janet played and
sang, the musicians simply stood still and listened. After about
twenty seconds, the drummer's head began to move in time. Ten
seconds later, the saxophonist came in with a first note. All three
fell into step with Janet, following her lead, a perfect quartet in
perfect time: the bass and drum became the backbone of the song,
the sax's runs were echoes of her melody. None of these musicians

had ever met before, but because they listened closely, they were able not only to support her but also to lift her song to new heights.

The illustration, incarnated, was obvious. As we talked with the CEOs over dinner afterward, they remarked that they had never connected musical behaviors to their work before. Work was work; music was simply entertainment. But now it seemed something more—a gateway into a new world of understanding themselves and their organizations, a world that was in the background until now. Listening is not a nice-to-have skill; it's core and essential. And with practice, it can be applied to every stage of entrepreneurship, from finding market opportunities to collaboration to connecting with audiences. Listen, notice, feel. Anticipate the possibilities that come from silence. And then start experimenting.

Interlude 1

We begin by heavily featuring Desmond Child's songbook and ending with Cage's "4'33"," performed by Italian composer Floraleda Sacchi. You can feel the audience's anticipation, unresolved, as the musician sits with her harp. Now that you know Desmond's songwriting strategy, do the titles tell the stories you expected?

HAPPY, Pharrell Williams
SILENCE (ILLENIUM REMIX), Marshmello, featuring Khalid
EXPRESS YOURSELF, N.W.A.
LA VIDA LOCA, Ricky Martin
TRAINWRECKS, Weezer
YOU GIVE LOVE A BAD NAME, Bon Jovi
I HATE MYSELF FOR LOVING YOU, Joan Jett
WAKING UP IN VEGAS, Katy Perry
HUMAN BEHAVIOR, Björk
ENJOY THE SILENCE, Depeche Mode
4'33", John Cage, performed by Floraleda Sacchi

Deep Listening: Listen to PJ Harvey's controversial *Hope Six Demolition Project*. The lyrics of the album are composed entirely from observational notes and quotes that Harvey picked up while traveling in Kosovo, Kabul, and Washington, DC. Then check out *Ultimate Care II* by Matmos, an album made entirely of sound recordings from a Whirlpool washing machine.

two
experimenting

Dare to Suck

I only have one rule in the studio, and it's this: dare to suck.

—Justin Timberlake

At the start of the Silicon Valley Bank event, mentioned in the previous chapter, we asked a question: "As CEO of your company, would you rather hire an athlete or a musician?" When we pose this question during our workshops, most executives reply that they would bank on a candidate with a background in sports.

We have nothing against athletes, of course! Michael was a high school basketball player, and Panos served in the military (and wakes up at 4 a.m. to work out every morning). But the question sets up an interesting dichotomy: athletic achievement has long been equated with leadership and being a team player, as well as with traits like grit, the will to win, and the commitment to practice repetitively until a move or play becomes muscle memory. Musicians, on the other hand, are often expected to be individualistic, undisciplined, and even dismissive of the corporate machine. Yes, there are many stories of hedonism, addiction, and rebellion in the annals of jazz, rock, country, and hip-hop. But is there any less of this behavior in the ledgers in collegiate and professional sports? Assumptions abound on both sides.

We contend that for every story of rock-and-roll excess, for every trashed hotel room or overdose, there are hundreds more of passion, hard work, and innovation. Dave Grohl, who rocketed to stardom as one of three members of Nirvana—a band known as a stripped-down benchmark of excess due in part to the addiction and suicide of front man Kurt Cobain—is famous for putting in hard work, showing up for gigs on time, and treating every paycheck as if it is the last one he will ever make. When a thousand Italians from a small town called Cesena covered his song "Learn to Fly" on a viral video, the fifteen-time Grammy winner replied in a video, in broken Italian, that his band the Foo Fighters would come to them for a concert and then delivered with a marathon twenty-seven-song show. When he fell off a stage in Sweden and broke his leg, he insisted on finishing the concert, seated in a chair with a medic holding his bandaged leg in place.

Grohl is exceptional, but he isn't the exception. We believe that musicians are uniquely equipped to adapt in an always-on, always-evolving world. They listen with open ears for opportunities, they can collaborate with new and unfamiliar teammates, and they bring both science and art to innovation. They know how to do more than run plays—they know how to play, to experiment.

Can't Stop the Feeling

Justin Timberlake found worldwide fame in the 1990s as a member of NSYNC, one of the best-selling boy bands in history. Since leaving the band to go solo, he has recorded four platinum-selling records and sold more than fifty-six million singles. His first two albums were the R&B-inspired *Justified* and *FutureSex/Love-Sounds*, which showcased his ability to merge soul, funk, and pop genres. In 2008, he took a four-year hiatus from recording music but continued to make hits, this time at movie theaters with roles in *The Social Network*, *Bad Teacher*, *Friends with Benefits*, and *In Time*. Since returning to the studio, he recorded a double album called *The 20/20 Experience*, an exploration of neo soul and 1970s rock, a chart-topping disco-inspired single "Can't Stop the Feeling," and *Man of the Woods*, which pairs Americana with hip-hop beats.

Panos sat down with Justin in May of 2019. The first thing that struck Panos was how tall Justin is; somehow in our minds, he was still the curly-haired, freckled kid from NSYNC. Yet here was a six-foot-one man in a print button-down shirt, a blazer, and cool Converse high tops, an embodied reminder of the fact that his career has spanned more than twenty years. The second thing we noticed is that he is quintessentially normal, down to earth, approachable, at ease with himself and others. Within minutes, it felt like we had known each other forever.

After a chat in the green room, Panos and Justin sat onstage in a crowded auditorium to talk for more than an hour about a wide range of topics—from his childhood in Memphis at the crossroads of musical influences from Chicago, Nashville, and Muscle Shoals, to winning Grammy Awards, to making movies. As it turns out, only a few days earlier the Songwriters Hall of Fame had announced that Justin would receive the Contemporary Icon Award at its fiftieth annual gala, so it's only natural that we also spent a good deal of time on writing songs.

The first song he wrote was as a preteen to persuade his parents to let him get an earring. He continued writing as a member of NSYNC but confessed that he lacked confidence in his abilities until working with Swedish überproducer Max Martin. Martin has produced more number-one hits than any songwriter other than Lennon and McCartney. He is legendary for his commitment to experimentation, pouring an inordinate amount of work into every song, exploring ideas repeatedly until he is satisfied. When they met, Justin was only sixteen years old.

"These were my music lessons, seeing that there weren't any rules, but there were guidelines that Max was very adamant about," he told Panos. "At such a young age, I was really lucky to be exposed to Max's tenacity in writing a song, to turn over every stone of every melody, to see what could sound wrong and right at the same time."

In the studio today, Justin applies the tenacious commitment he learned from Martin. "The key is to keep writing," he said. "I have only one rule in the studio, and it's this: dare to suck. You may have a great idea in your head as somebody's playing a riff on the guitar. Don't hold it in. I actually find myself saying out loud: 'OK guys, I'm going to dare to suck, but what about this?'"

Taking a song from idea to completion is a relentless commitment to trying ideas—testing and proving them or discarding them. "There are no wrong answers when it comes to creating art because each idea is only going to lead you to what feels good," he told Panos. "And for you to connect to other people, it has to feel good to you first. When a song comes out, it's mostly because I can live with it at that point. If a song of mine comes on the radio, I can tell you what I could have done better, what line I could have sung better. It's not meant to be perfect, but you do have to feel like it's great because that's what is going to give you confidence to take it out into the world."

Unlike athletic or scientific experimentation, musical experimentation doesn't start with a research plan and a fixed method. The more options that an artist tries, the more likely she is to discover an idea worth building upon. Justin has applied this approach not only to songwriting but also to exploring new paths and ideas in his career like acting. During the interview, Panos asked Justin about a passage from his autobiography *Hindsight & All the Things I Can't See in Front of Me.*

Sometimes it feels like everybody wants you to stay right where you are. Everybody's always looking for a definition, a classification, a rule. They want to pin you down so they can understand you. They want you to make it easy for them. They want you to walk in a straight line. I say walk your own line.

"I don't want to do the same thing twice," he told Panos. "I want to continue to learn and be creative. Sometimes I can be impossible with myself, and that's OK too. But I'm still making things, and I don't move until I see it, until it all starts to make sense."

Chopping This and Doing That and Using the Box of Tricks

Let's take a closer look at musical experimentation in action. After all, it can take many forms and flavors, depending on the artist or even the particular album in development. In early 2020, we traveled to Havering-atte-Bower, a village outside London, to talk with Imogen Heap.

Imogen is a Grammy Award–winning singer-songwriter who also achieved fame as a producer for Taylor Swift's landmark record *1989* and as the composer of the soundtrack for Broadway's *Harry Potter and the Cursed Child*. As if this were not enough to keep her busy, she also collaborated with technology innovator Kelly Snook to invent the Mi.Mu smart gloves, which began as an experiment in her home studio in 2010 and then evolved into a full-fledged product over the past decade. The high-tech gloves enable musicians to express and articulate music in new ways, both in the studio or onstage, or to compose and play songs, using only their hands. When a musician pulls Mi.Mu gloves on, she can reach into musical software, as it were, with simple gestures. Raising or lowering one hand changes the pitch. Opening your palms wide starts a thumping beat. Pinching fingers, chopping, and slapping creates loops or reverb. A performer can construct an entire song, track upon track, without ever touching an instrument.

Imogen provided prototypes to beatboxers, vocalists, and visual artists to expand their use; pop star Ariana Grande used them onstage during her 2015 world tour. The gloves even open new doors for musicians with disabilities like cerebral palsy who might struggle to play the guitar, piano, or other instruments. This real-world research and development gave her the confidence to release them to the public in late 2020.

She also has undertaken a new venture, Mycelia, using blockchain technology to identify all of a musician's past and present works, streamline payments to musicians, and enable new kinds of collaboration.

"I'm lucky to have time and space to experiment, to try to get to something original, or maybe just something fun, or to try a different kind of music making," she told us. "The first example of when I realized I could do that was when I wrote 'Hide and Seek.' It was my first time trying to make an album from start to finish on my own, and I had been in the studio for nearly a month. Very late one night my computer's motherboard blew up. I lost everything that I'd been doing for the past three weeks because I hadn't saved anything."

Rather than give up and go home, Imogen decided that she didn't want to leave the studio on a bad note. A friend had loaned her a digital harmonizer called a Digitech Workstation, but it had been sitting unused on the radiator.

"I thought: I'll just plug that in. A piece of equipment that was new to me, with no expectation that anything in particular would happen. And the first thing that came out of my mouth was the words: 'Where are we? What the hell is going on?' It was just a nice, improvised moment."

On the recording, the only sound that listeners can hear is her affected voice. All of the harmonies are the result of the notes Imogen touches on the keyboard, telling the harmonizer which notes to make her voice appear to sing. She started tweaking the degree of harmonization, reacting to the chord inversions, finding a balance between her natural voice and the synthesized versions of it.

"I didn't overthink it. I did a quick take, chopping this and doing that and using the box of tricks—then left it, coming back to it later and thinking: oh, this is great, that's great, that's rubbish. If I'm singing a melody, in the back of my mind I think: the melody is wrong, but the tone of voice isn't. Or I play something on the piano and realize that even though it shouldn't be on the piano, there's something about that interval that I really like."

After that first session of experimentation, Imogen estimates that the song was three-quarters finished; it only took another two weeks for her to cut sections of the song and round out the lyrics. When she played it for friends and fellow musicians, many recommended that she add a baseline or beats, but Imogen declined.

"I felt like I was self-indulging in this a cappella piece, this weird bit of music that I thought nobody would like but that I really loved. I felt like it was an accomplishment, something I'd never done before, verging on original, that didn't sound like anything I'd ever heard."

Imogen put "Hide and Seek" on the record, and a producer working for the Fox television show *The O.C.* included it on their soundtrack at the height of the show's popularity. In the years since, the song has appeared on more than a dozen soundtracks, ranging from *So You Think You Can Dance*, to *CSI: Miami* and *The L Word*, to films, including *The Last Kiss* and *The Town*, and has sold more than 650,000 copies.

Always experimenting, always exploring new ideas. On the day that we sat down together, Imogen had just completed an experimental side project for Stephen Hoggett, the choreographer for *Harry Potter and the Cursed Child*. Hoggett had emailed Imogen videos of four different dancers moving to the same soundtrack, but he sent it without an audio file. His request? For Imogen to compose a song inspired by the dance, rather than the other way around.

"I try to take on things that scare me a bit, or where I think: I can't do that. As soon as I feel that, I think: OK, that's the reason to do it."

For Hoggett's videos, Imogen began with an analytical approach, trying to find a beat. She went through the videos frame by frame, measuring the dancers' feet and distance, searching for hints of a rhythm.

"Then I thought: that's silly, I should just hit play on the video. As I watched, the first thing I played was a chord, a long, really nice chord. Then three chords, without letting it reach the tonic, all while asking myself: what are the dancers trying to say? One of them was shaking her hands beside her head, as if she were having a breakdown, then she went a bit angular, then had a moment of freedom where she was running. And I sang what I felt: 'You're working too hard.' The whole song basically became that: you're working too hard."

She showed us the video while playing her score. As the dancer moves in a rehearsal room, Imogen begins with layers of her own voice rising and falling, shifts into a bridge of snaps and synthesizer before resolving into a long and lovely piano melody, and then returning to her voice, simple and natural and graceful.

"I don't feel like I understood the dance in any special way; I just started playing the music, heard the first chord, and built on the first thing that came out of my mouth."

Hoggett felt otherwise. By email, his response was: "Imogen, my God, this is incredible. Watching this, I'm assured that you understand me in ways that are immaculate. To then make the understanding musical like that, I fully understand why I feel symbiotic to your work."

As Imogen said, she recognizes that she is in a fortunate space, lucky to have room to experiment and play. But we all recognize that giving ourselves this room to explore ideas, to try and try again, is not only beneficial for artists, it's also good for business.

Room for Play

Ella Joy Meir is an Israeli songwriter and computer programmer who now lives in Brooklyn. In 2017, *Billboard* magazine wrote about Meir and her band, Iris Lune: "A soaring and ethereal collection of songs each build from their own miniature tales, with a clear mashup of both Eastern and Western musical influences infused into each."

Over the past three years, she has written original music for Facebook and Instagram, for royalty-free use in videos created and posted by its users. When we asked her about writing songs for Facebook users and how it frees her up to explore new sounds, she told us that one of her favorite parts of being a student was that she was asked to create new songs every week. After graduating, she taught music to make a living but had to find time on her own to write. As a composer for Facebook, she gets to do both.

Over the last three years, she's contributed around ninety songs. "A lot of pop and folk singer-songwriter tracks but also Middle Eastern, house, trance, ambient, glitch, a cappella, and classical. I'm always open to diving into new genres, pinpointing what makes a style what it is then adding my own spin to it, learning as I go."

This kind of free experimentation made us think of Foley rooms in sound design studios. A Foley room is an acoustically tuned space used for reproducing everyday sounds to be added to films and video. The pit can be filled with leaves; it can be used for breaking glass or pouring water over waterproof microphones. Where the room gets really fun, however, is in the hands of sound effects artists. The noise that a knife makes stabbing a watermelon becomes part of the score of a horror film; the hum of an old film projector becomes the swoosh of a laser sword. These artists repurpose an everyday tool in a new way—a strategy that has also led to significant breakthroughs in pop music.

Digital tools have opened up new opportunities for experimentation, but musicians have been experimenting with sounds and what music means, how it is created, throughout history. Daphne Oram, a sound engineer and founder of the BBC's Radiophonic Workshop, became a pioneer of electronic music when she manipulated the speed of recorded music during playback. For her 1950 composition "Still Point," Oram took records playing at various speeds, recorded the sound on tape, and then incorporated it into the performance of a live orchestra. It was the world's first example of real-time transformation of prerecorded sound, the precursor to trip-hop groups like Portishead and Massive Attack nearly fifty years later.

Inspired by a trick he learned from a session musician, Led Zeppelin guitarist Jimmy Page mesmerized concert crowds by using a cello bow to play "Dazed and Confused" and "How Many Times" on his guitar, creating a sound like a Tibetan singing bowl. Today, Jonsi Birgisson employs the technique to give Icelandic art rock band Sigur Rós its otherworldly sound.

Theodore Livingstone, also known as Grand Wizzard Theodore, created "scratching" in 1975 by holding a vinyl record with his fingers and then shifting it back and forth on the platter. With two turntables, he could interject sounds from one record into the music of the other. After toying with the technique at home for months, he debuted his idea in 1977 at an outdoor party, and a seminal component of early hip-hop was born.

Experimenting is a mindset that is underpinned with curiosity and discovery. Whether it leads to new insights or entirely new creations, experimentation is inherently optimistic, rooted in the belief that something interesting will come from exploration, from playing.

Happy Accidents

Sometimes the best experiments happen accidentally. In 1951, blues pianist Ike Turner and his band the Kings of Rhythm recorded "Rocket 88," which many consider to be the first-ever rock-and-roll song. Most of the song was straightforward rhythm and blues, but the sound of the guitar was exciting and different. This trademark sound came about literally by accident.

Driving to a recording session with Sam Phillips in Memphis, the band had crammed their equipment into the back of a car. One of the guitar amplifiers was a tube amplifier, sending sound through a large glass cone that was quite delicate. The amp toppled over en route, cracking its tubes. Rather than spending several days and precious money to repair it, the band attempted a DIY fix, stuffing the cone with newspaper to keep its broken pieces in place. The paper muffled and distorted the guitar's sound into a warm, fuzzy tone.

After hearing "Rocket 88," other guitarists started looking for ways to break their own equipment. Link Wray punched holes in his amp's speaker cover, and his groundbreaking, heavily distorted instrumental track "Rumble" gave us the world's first popular use of power chords. His song was seen as so new, so provocative that it was banned from America's radio waves—the only instrumental song ever banned in our country's history. Fifteen years later, Jimi Hendrix perfected guitar distortion and made it central to rock music.

Of course, this kind of experimentation-turned-application is not limited to music. Play-Doh, a staple of childhood for nearly a century, first saw the light of day as a product created to clean coal residue off wallpaper. But after World War II, most homes shifted away from coal-based heating in favor of natural gas or electricity, and the putty fell out of demand, until an executive's wife saw its potential as a modeling clay for kids. The Slinky was designed as a spring to stabilize sensitive equipment on ships; its potential as a toy only became obvious when one fell off a shelf, stepping down in a series of arcs to a stack of books, a tabletop, and the floor. These products and many more—from penicillin to Post-it adhesive notes—only saw the light of day because their inventors viewed them as happy accidents and recognized their new potential.

Free Exploration

We live in an era obsessed with innovation. Yet ironically, most companies lack enthusiasm for giving employees the freedom to play. Far too often, play is seen as a dangerous recipe for wasting time and money; instead, staff, studios, and consultants are pressured to invent new-to-the-world products and services on compressed time lines with limited resources, in isolated back rooms with unfortunate names like "Creative Thinking Room" or "Innovation Lab." Time is money, and money shouldn't be wasted, so rapid relevance rules the day.

Think of how many start-ups, in an effort to stand against this sort of corporate culture, proudly show potential candidates and new recruits their video game centers or ball pits in their offices. This is a well-intentioned but misguided idea because the greatest benefit of play is not in letting employees take a break from work but rather integrating play into the research and development (aka creative) process. Prioritizing play is not antioptimization or antiefficiency. It might not lead to immediate breakthroughs with an obvious connection to the project at hand, but it's still worthwhile because it gives people space to create work that is more innovative, more exciting, and more connected to the parts of life that they really care about.

In fact, the belief that experimentation is a means to an end and must happen quickly and efficiently is a relatively recent phenomenon, even in corporate cultures. From 1951 to 1959, Marvin Kelly was director of Bell Labs. For years on end, he deliberately did not ask what his scientists and engineers were exploring, developing, creating. He wanted to give them complete freedom to explore ideas and define their own processes—to the point that when they presented their products, he didn't even ask about their potential applications. Kelly knew that experimentation is the foundation of great design and engineering, and he was right: during his tenure, Bell Labs invented the transistor, the cellular phone, the laser, and the communications satellite.

To dive more into the topic, we turned to Steve Vai. Growing up as young guitarists, we idolized Steve: a three-time Grammy winner, he is most famous for his virtuoso prowess on stage, backing Frank

Zappa, David Lee Roth, Whitesnake, Mary J. Blige, and Ozzy Os-
bourne. Steve stands out from other heavy metal shredders who play
fast and with incredible precision yet with no emotion; his playing
is faster and more precise yet it has incredible feeling, even warmth.
When he was honored with the Les Paul Award in 2012, the National Association of Music Merchants (NAMM) Foundation said:
"Steve Vai dedicated his talents to creatively advance the language of
music. While many artists fit easily into a single category, Steve Vai
remains unclassifiable. He is a musical alchemist of the highest order."

Yet Steve is perhaps most famous not only for his breathtaking
solos but also for designing the best-selling signature series guitar
of all time: the Ibanez JEM. Guitar manufacturers have a long
history of issuing signature editions, branded with the names of
famous musicians, with little change to their mass-produced models. These signature edition models might offer different woods,
better pickups, advanced tuners, a range of colors, and, of course,
the actual signature of a celebrity inlaid in the headstock. But
Steve wanted more.

"Creating the JEM was an innocent, joyful, enthusiastic freedom of creative experimentation," he told us. "There was no expectation whatsoever for the future of the guitar, for it to make a
lot of money. Sometimes when you are creating with an agenda,
it gets in the way. I had no agenda. I had these guitars built independently, for myself."

When he started on the project, he was touring with David
Lee Roth and felt that his Fender Stratocaster, with twenty-two
frets, was underwhelming. As a guitarist whose fingers could find
the high notes with incredible dexterity he longed for a longer
neck so that he could play two full octaves on each string.

"I wanted twenty-four frets. And I wanted a Stratocaster style,
but it had to be sexier than a Strat, because they look pedestrian to
me. So I drew up something and had a luthier cut it out."

Once he could reach the high notes, Steve still wasn't satisfied. He wanted to be able to stretch the strings, to bend notes

dramatically sharp. The guitar's body prevented him from doing this, so he cut deep into the guitar body, giving space for his hands to work. Finally, he wanted a monkey grip—inspired by the handle on a horseback riding saddle, so he could theatrically twirl and spin the guitar during shows.

"I sent out the prototype design to all of the guitar manufacturers who had contacted me and said: 'Whoever makes what I want the best, that's the one I'll play, the one that will have my name on it.' Inevitably, most of them sent back one of their standard guitars with my name on it and a couple of little changes. I couldn't understand why they would do that, when I had told them what I wanted."

Ibanez, however, came back with a fully realized version of Steve's design, including the additional frets, the cutaway and monkey grip, and a palm rest next to the bridge tremolo—everything he had requested. And, as it turns out, both Steve and Ibanez were onto something: in the thirty years since it was created, millions of JEM guitars have sold. While many other vanity project guitars have been created for rock stars, then discontinued, for three decades the various models of the JEM have dominated the market.

It's possible for research and development in any company to feel the free exploration that Steve describes. But how do you set off on an experimental journey? This is a familiar conversation in the world of design. Designers have codified their process of consistently creating experiments that move a product, a system, or an experience toward outcomes that resonate with consumers. "Design thinking," in fact, has become shorthand for a way to share the methods and mindsets of designers with the broader world of business to experiment and build upon ideas together. One design-thinking practice, closely related to experimentation, is to start with an existing product or service and break it down into its most basic components. Pick them up one at a time to see what else they might do. Suddenly, a camera can be mounted on a mobile phone. Wheels can be put on a suitcase. A handle can be built into a guitar.

In 2013, a pair of young businessmen, TJ Parker and Elliot Cohen, set up shop in the IDEO Cambridge office as its first Start-up in Residence. TJ had grown up in his family's New Hampshire pharmacy and had a vision for a prescription home-delivery service called PillPack. They had developed industry insight and a robotic pill-sorting technology, but they wanted to create an experience that didn't exist in the pharmacy space.

"We had a strong hunch that the service would be appealing but were struggling with how to build trust when it comes to something as important and personal as prescription medication," said Colin Raney, an IDEO fellow who became PillPack's chief marketing officer. "People don't think of themselves as having a pharmacy problem; they just struggle to take their medication and don't think of their pharmacy as making this easier. We started testing ideas around how to talk about convenience, without getting bogged down in the inherent complications of prescriptions and insurance."

From prior research, they knew people were not aware of the different prescription delivery options; in fact, they didn't think about their pharmacy at all unless they needed a prescription filled. So a core team of five IDEO designers started playing with messaging ideas by setting up a booth in a local mall. For three consecutive weekends, the team tested a range of messages—changing booth signage and verbiage, switching out price points and subscription models, presenting different iterations of packaging—to see what resonated with potential customers. On the first weekend, they focused on the convenience of medication sorting and home delivery; on the second they shifted focus to having a pharmacist always available through a mobile app; on the third they talked about creating a safer pharmacy. People reacted most positively to the benefits of home delivery, so saving time and making things easy became key components of PillPack's product messaging.

According to Colin, this team-based, iterative experience has had an incredible impact on the company's culture. "When you build a culture of experimentation," he said, "you create constant curiosity around how things could improve. Teams start to approach problems differently. You accept that there are no silver bullets and that some ideas will fail, but you'll learn from the failure.

> In 2017, we needed to scale our business. We knew that our customers watch a lot of television, so we decided to try our hand at commercials. Typically, a company hires an advertising agency, who develops a concept and engages a production company to create the ad. It's an expensive process, and there's no guarantee that it will work. It felt wrong to hand over a project this important to someone else and hope for the best, so we thought about creating our own ads. Over the years, we had gotten pretty good at creative video content, but this was a much bigger gamble. In the end, we turned the project into a series of experiments, writing four different commercials, testing different ideas in each spot, and hired a small production company to help with the video. All of this cost much less than the typical process of creating a commercial, and we learned tons about what works (and what doesn't). We've repeated this process, and over two years have aired thirty different commercials, with television becoming one of our most important marketing channels. Framing this project as a bunch of smaller experiments allowed us to learn and improve as we went.

In 2018, Amazon acquired PillPack for $753 million. This was itself an experiment, by Amazon; health is a new frontier for the megacompany, and PillPack was a way for them to test the waters.

Whether you are an innovator, business leader, musician, or all of these combined, the commitment to exploration and discovery through experimentation can make the difference between being another face in the crowd or standing above it.

Interlude 2

Modified gear, affected sounds, unusual song structures, and misappropriated tools define this experimental mixtape. Watch for the sonic textures that these artists introduced through playfulness and improvisation. Notice the cello-bow-played guitar in the middle of "Dazed and Confused" and discover it again with Sigur Rós.

THREE SINGLE SOUNDS TAKEN IN CANON IV, Daphne Oram
ROCKET 88, Kings of Rhythm
FILTHY, Justin Timberlake
GANGBUSTERS, Grand Wizzard Theodore
DAZED AND CONFUSED, Led Zeppelin
ALIEN WATER KISS, Steve Vai
SÆGLÓPUR, Sigur Rós
HIDE AND SEEK, Imogen Heap
I'M BECOMING, Steve Vai
KOLN 2008 DJ SET 2, Grand Wizzard Theodore

Deep Listening: Check out "Ba Ba Ti Ki Di Do" by Sigur Rós, a selection of live, improvised music performed for Merce Cunningham's postmodern dance *Split Sides*.

three
collaborating

Merge to Make

I think I wrote a good hook, I think I had a good idea . . . but now when I listen back to the demo, it sounds different because she contextualized the song . . . it has deeper meaning. 99% of the world will hear those words and associate them with Beyoncé.

—Ezra Koenig

Have you ever found yourself on a project, unsure of exactly where you are going or how to get there, but in good company? That's how a collaboration should feel. You start with an idea that is so ambitious, so new, or so different from what you have done before that you are acutely aware that you can't succeed on your own. Other people's skill sets and talents are needed to pull it off.

There's a sense of fumbling forward in the dark but also that there's strength in numbers.

The Solid Sound Music Festival is held in the Berkshires, a few miles from where our families live in the Boston area. Founded by Wilco, a Grammy Award–winning American band known for exploring a wide range of sounds from alternative country to lush orchestral pop to autumnal folk, Solid Sound is one of our favorite festivals. On a warm June night in 2017, Michael and his wife and kids were invited to an after-party by friends of Wilco.

We piled into our Volkswagen van and drove deep into the Berkshires. But this was not a typical after-party: there was no red carpet or photo booth, no canapés or DJ. Instead, when we arrived at the location, we found only a construction site with concrete footers and plywood structures on the banks of the Hoosic River. As it turned out, the after-party was actually a christening: the surprise launch of a new hotel called Tourists, created to bring strangers together around shared experiences.

After a dinner served from a makeshift kitchen covered with a tarp, the hosts appeared with a lantern and led our group into the woods. We walked quietly across a steel-framed, state-of-the-art suspension bridge, seemingly out of place in the quiet wooded surroundings, along a freshly macheted path until we arrived at a small, newly constructed chapel. It was little more than a skeletal pergola bathed in two spotlights, draped by a hundred chimes suspended from ropes. A hybrid place of meditation art and musical instruments, carved out of the surrounding darkness.

The moment was disorienting and surreal but also beautiful. We all stood without speaking, taking in the scene, the calls of tree frogs and the distant roar of the river. Then two figures stepped forward, one with a guitar and one with mallets, and the air filled with the ring of arpeggiated chords and the ethereal rhythm of hammered chimes. From the woods behind them, at first as a murmur but growing in power, a trumpet began playing a melody. We were at first witnesses but then participants, playing the chimes along with the artists.

A few days later, we sat down with Wilco bassist John Stirratt to talk about the project.

"Before launching Tourists, I never thought of myself as a businessman, much less a hotel owner," John said. "I grew up in the '80s, in underground music, and we distrusted business. I guess it was still punk to do that," he told us, laughing. But after a quarter century of traveling across America and around the world with the band, he noticed a trend. Small cities and larger towns had changed between tours; places he had been before were remarkably different a couple of years later. Small boutique hotels and coffee shops were popping up, serving quality products and reshaping these landscapes.

"I saw how people in the restaurant and hospitality industry were actually changing lives, particularly with food and coffee. They were bringing a romance to their work, making it an art form, and growing from a few founders to hundreds of employees. This demystified the business side for me. I saw the same counterculture and kinship that I knew in music."

An entrepreneurial idea started to take shape: How could he help bring people together and bring this sort of focused, intentional renewal to the small town of North Adams, Massachusetts? As John thought of his touring travels, two hotels particularly resonated with his sensibilities: Hotel San José and Hotel Saint Cecilia, both in Austin, Texas.

"I have the same feeling checking into the San José as I do listening to a Miles Davis record for the fiftieth time," he said. "It's a visceral experience, a feeling of possibility."

So he enlisted Lisa Reile, former general manager of both properties, as a consultant; she helped connect him with real estate developer Ben Svenson, media entrepreneur Scott Stedman, and brewery owner Eric Kerns.

For John, it was familiar, like being in a band: "Friends in British bands tell me that being in a band is like being in a club. They don't trust anyone outside their circle. But it's different in America. Here it's a thing to have extended collaboration, a larger community. As partners in this project, we were creating a dream hotel, like writing a song you have never heard before."

Here was a man who once had strong negative feelings about business applying his musical instincts and approaching a start-up as an art project. To hear John describe their process, it was a bit like a jam session, often loose and informal, with an almost impromptu feel. Part practice, part community, a jam session is an opportunity to play together without predetermined arrangements or sheet music. When participating, each musician knows the importance of leaving space for others, when to step up and when to step back. If one person is always soloing, turning up their own volume, then the music turns to mush. A great collaboration is about trusting one another, using creative fluency to be fluid in roles, and so creating a whole that is greater than the sum of its parts. John told us that with Tourists, trust was the foundation of what the team built, as solid as the concrete footers. Beginning with hand sketches, each brought their own tools and ideas: architecture mixed with service, food, geography, and ecology, as well as careful attention to the history and character of North Adams.

Tourists opened in the summer of 2018. It is a spare place of calm in the surrounding fifty-five acres of woods, featuring minimalist architecture, meandering paths, honest materials, and an engaging staff. An onsite restaurant, Loom, was founded by James Beard Award–winning chef Cortney Burns, with the intention of knitting together the cultures and foods native to North Adams, in a gathering place where people break bread and share time together.

Every detail has been designed by the cofounders to create warmth and resonance: from the soft aromas of coffee, palo santo, and leather to the guest rooms outfitted with white oak furniture and floors with bright white feather duvets on the beds. Small delights abound: vintage postcards from the surrounding region, a field guide to the grounds, hand-carved bath soaps.

One particularly unique touch is Tourists Radio, the hotel's shortwave FM station, which streams from Tivoli Audio Model One radios in each room. We assumed this soundtrack was John's contribution to the atmosphere, but to our surprise, we learned that Eric first suggested it as an experiment for the Solid Sound Festival. When the hotel began taking shape, the radio station felt like a natural fit, so John riffed on Eric's idea and started programming the airwaves.

"I've always hated how hotels crank up popular music at night to create a rave scene," he told us. "At Tourists, we don't do that. I don't want people to recognize any of the songs; the whole point is for the music to take you to a new place. I had to get a feeling for the place and its own life and then choose music to match."

Dialing in this vibe took John a while to figure out. At first, he drew on his early counterculture roots and chose classic bands like The Minutemen and Hüsker Dü, from independent labels like SST Records. The spirit was right for the project, but the sound wasn't. So he went back to a blank page, selecting music to match the atmosphere that Lisa and the staff had created. The resulting playlist is a mash-up of outsider folk, dream pop, and classic rock and hip hop—all with an ethos that feels simultaneously distant and comforting.

This pattern of handing off an idea from one member of the creative team to another for development worked in both directions. John even contributed to the interior design of the lodge.

"I proposed a sofa to the group: a Brazilian modern Lafer that I thought would work. I was so into it, but of course Julie Pearson was able to find something even more rare and fitting for the space. Over and over, the team was all in the same general ballpark, that it was refinement of an idea in most cases, instead of sharp turns."

Reflecting back on the chapel-christening ceremony, John felt that it embodied the entire spirit of the project. "That evening let us occupy the space where the hotel would eventually be, bringing people together in a proof-of-concept of how this place really feels. There was something superspecial about it; we all felt it, and it made us want to proceed with a bigger version of what became Tourists." That vision was key to making this collaboration work. Even though the players were from such different walks of life, they were able to find a shared rhythm through a shared dream.

Collaboration Is Pursuit

When Miles Davis was eighteen years old, he famously moved from St. Louis to New York in a search for legendary virtuoso trumpeter and singer Dizzy Gillespie. Davis was already wildly talented and could have held his own with any jazz legend, but he wanted to play with the person he admired most. The draw was Gillespie's talent, his uniqueness, his jagged, audacious departures from written chord sequences—all of which were very different from Davis's lyrical, personal, and introspective style. A 1960 edition of the UK's *Guardian* newspaper said: "There could not be a greater contrast between Davis' and Gillespie's approach. Where Gillespie looked his audience over, laughed at it and defied it to understand what he was doing, Davis seems unaware that he has an audience. His effects are aimed at himself and at those who play with him."

What drove one trumpeter to pursue another? It was the opportunity for discovery, a desire to learn, and a desire to grow together. This kind of teamwork is not about coming together to win, to chase a sports or military-style victory. It is about merging to make, leading and following as modes. The old image of an artist or entrepreneur as a lone wolf, hacking his personal vision out of the wilderness, is not always the best way to get the best results. Sometimes it takes a team.

If any musician working today has the capacity to act like a lone wolf, it is Beyoncé. In 2003 she broke with her band Destiny's

Child to pursue a solo career, and in the years since has become one of the most successful musicians of all time, selling more than 118 million records. The Recording Industry Association of America recognized her as the top certified artist of the 2000s. Without question, Queen Bey has the talent and drive to stand alone.

Yet her 2016 album *Lemonade* is one of the most ambitious collaborative albums in music history. *Rolling Stone* magazine called it "the ultimate collage, a potpourri of competing sounds, images, and ideas, plucked from a dizzying variety of far-flung sources." Most of its songs have at least three songwriters; some have upward of ten. The list of more than one hundred contributors includes big names like Kendrick Lamar, Jack White of the White Stripes, and the Weeknd, as well as indie rock collaborators like Vampire Weekend, Animal Collective, and Father John Misty. Songs on the album dabble in hard rock, country, reggae, rap, and funk, as well as R&B.

Beyoncé's approach on *Lemonade* went well beyond typical pop collaborations, where guest artists are invited to contribute a loop, a lick, or a bridge vocal. Instead, she asked her cocreators for their ideas and then built one idea on top of another. The resulting songs are unlike anything she had recorded before and demonstrate how far her talent extends, as well as the extent of her trust in other talents.

Let's look at one track, the hit song "Hold Up," as an example. In 2003, indie rock band the Yeah Yeah Yeahs released a song called "Maps," which included the line: "Wait, they don't love you like I love you." The song went on to be ranked among the top songs of the 2000s by *NME*, *Pitchfork*, and *Rolling Stone*. Eight years later, Ezra Koenig, front man of the indie rock band Vampire Weekend, posted a revision of the line on Twitter: "Hold up . . . they don't love u like I love u." A few more years on, Koenig was working with Diplo, a producer who has worked with Madonna, Justin Bieber, and Snoop Dogg, and the pair wrote a melody loosely based on the line from "Maps": "Hold up, they don't love you like I love you. There's no other god above you, what a wicked way to treat a man who loves you." The song was originally intended to be for Vampire Weekend, but Koenig decided to send it to Beyoncé instead. And like Miles pursuing Dizzy, this started a domino effect, a dizzying back-and-forth between creative icons, all of whom are credited as songwriters on the track.

Beyoncé first sent the track to Emile Haynie, a producer who has worked with rappers, including Eminem and Kid Cudi. Unexpectedly, Haynie suggested that they invite Josh Tillman to assist with lyrics. The choice was surprising: Tillman occupies a vastly different musical space from Beyoncé, having risen to fame as the drummer for Fleet Foxes and later performing as the musical prankster and self-described "authentically bogus" stage character Father John Misty. Even though he was asked to contribute a few lyrics, Tillman spent an exhausting week creating reams of verses, melodies, and refrains, most of which he was convinced would end up on the cutting-room floor.

Instead, Beyoncé sent an instrumental version of Tillman's chorus to British songwriter MNEK, with very limited instructions. "The great thing about her team," MNEK said, "was that they were just like, 'We asked you to be a part of this because we like what you do. So just do your thing.'" So MNEK did his thing, writing an entire song around that chorus. Beyoncé particularly loved one specific section, which became the bridge of the song.

She then gathered up all of her favorite bits and pieces from each contributor and sent them to Brooklyn DJ and rapper MeLo-X. MeLo-X had first come to Beyoncé's attention several years earlier when he remixed five of her songs and posted them on sharing platforms like SoundCloud and YouTube. Even though Beyoncé's label had repeatedly had the remixes removed from the sharing platforms, citing copyright violation, Beyoncé liked what she heard, invited MeLo-X on tour, and made him a frequent writing partner.

"I really just know my side of it. It was pretty much, maybe 50 percent complete when I heard it, and I just wrote a bunch of things from my perspective," MeLo-X said. "A bunch of harmonies, a bunch of different layers, and she kept a lot of that in."

In all, fifteen people contributed to "Hold Up." Each was given a songwriting credit, including the Yeah Yeah Yeah's Karen O, who had penned the line that started it all. *Pitchfork* called the song "a delirious flight of fancy. The music has no weight, no place, no time—a calypso dream heard through walls and generations."

In the years since the album's release, scholarly articles and academic treatises have been written on *Lemonade*. Many of them focus on the album's depiction of a woman at a crossroads, after discovering that her husband has been unfaithful. What do you do when life gives you lemons? In attempting to process the real-life infidelity of her husband, Beyoncé created a bold statement of independence that is also a meditation on the complications of marriage and relationships and how we connect with and miss each other as human beings. In the end, *Lemonade* is a picture of the restorative power of community. Her musical collaborations not only embodied this vision artistically, they made it possible for her to share it with the world.

The Skeleton Key

Pharrell Williams started his music career in high school, winning a talent show that led to a record deal. Even though the deal fell apart, Pharrell had his first exposure to writing and producing songs. In the years following, he collaborated with Kanye West on "Number One," Snoop Dogg on "Drop It Like It's Hot," and Gwen Stefani on "Can I Have It Like That."

However, with typical humility, he says that he did not consider himself a producer until Daft Punk's 2013 global hit "Get Lucky." He wrote the song for the French electronic music duo, assuming they would have someone else record the final vocals. Rather than re-recording the vocals, the band used Pharrell's track on the song's final version.

"I was just so freshly shocked," Pharrell said. "I didn't know I was going to stay on the song."

Building upon this success, he reached new heights as a producer, working with CeeLo Green and Azealia Banks, as well as with Robin Thicke on "Blurred Lines." In the midaughts, he pivoted out of the music industry to start a collaboration with Adidas. Pharrell's interest in Adidas was rooted in the products themselves. As a young teen in Virginia Beach, he bopped to Run DMC's 1986 legendary rap track "My Adidas"; the triple-stripe Superstar sneakers were ubiquitous on the block. Adidas is a brand of the people, he said, and just as importantly, it dovetails with his own sense that genre barricades are made to be broken. Much as he has crossed lines of musical genres in his career, seeing the ability of artistic disruption to create new sounds, he applied the same thinking to his clothing lines.

Footwear and apparel brands have long engaged with sports and music celebrities for endorsements, and Adidas has deliberately positioned itself as a brand for creators. Collaborations go far deeper than copromotion or shared cultural capital; changemakers like Pharrell are actively involved in product design.

Torben Schumacher, general manager of Adidas, said: "We've always seen our role as one of a connector—championing the creative mindset. As a brand, we've been able to provide a platform for creative minds that they may not otherwise have access to. It's been through these authentic connections that we've been invited into the conversations that are shaping culture."

Pharrell said: "Just like anyone else, I wore both [designer clothing and streetwear]. It's not like I discovered anything. We just did a whole lot of arguing to get people to see that they were putting these partitions up. If you look at what pop culture was doing on its own, beyond what you could get at a retail store or a boutique, everyone was always mixing it up."

Their first collaboration, released in 2014, was a two-piece collection that included a revision of the iconic Stan Smith sneaker, first introduced in the 1970s, and a Superstar jacket. More than a dozen collections followed, including a partnership with both

Chanel and Adidas, creating a custom pair of Adidas NMD sneakers that now resell for more than $12,000. Pharrell's Hu line, short for "human," includes a fourteen-piece apparel collection and five variations on sneakers, drawing inspiration from the many shades and variations of people's skin color—deliberately designed to spark conversation around racial and cultural barriers.

"Hu is about the recognition and celebration of different colors, spirituality and cultures," he has said. "The point is to highlight the differences so people can realize that despite all those differences, we are all basically the same. . . . Our goal is to tell many different stories. As society evolves, we realize the blend of cultures is an enriching thing. We are learning that we can celebrate our differences and not let them divide us."

For Pharrell, each of these projects and collaborations come from the same place, and all are rooted in music, his "skeleton key."

"I treat all projects just like I do music. You have a collection of sounds, and it's like your own Lego block building system where you just sort of color coordinate. . . . First of all, you have an idea, you have something that you feel like is missing. And from there you sort of figure out what the schematic is going to be, the blueprint, and then you sort of color-code it and build it. And I find that making a chair is not really different from making a song. There's a hook, there's legs, there's the seat, there's the verses, the hinges or the screws or the glue is the chord structure.

"You're pretty much using different materials, but it's the same thing. You have an idea, you create your blueprint, your schematic. You fabricate it, you build it, you set it free; you let the world see it. Whether it's a song or a chair, it's the same thing."

The "it" here is a creative mindset, and Pharrell uses it brilliantly. Although he is not a trained designer, he approaches collaboration as if he were. He sees the potential of an idea and leverages that idea through the skill sets of talented partners and teammates.

"Pharrell connects with everyone in the room and encourages them to think bigger than product," said Adidas SVP of Global

Design Nic Galway. "He takes inspiration from everywhere, whether it be globally or across the brand, and wants to create change with everything he does."

"Those different modes and different ways of expressing yourself use a different language and lexicon," Pharrell told us. "The subject matter changes, but you yourself aren't any different. Each just happens to be a mode of expression."

Yesterday, Love Was Such an Easy Game to Play

When it comes to collaborators, choosing the right partners is essential. In early 2020, we spoke with American singer, songwriter, and chart-topper John Legend. One of only a handful of people to have achieved an EGOT—winning an Emmy, Grammy, Oscar, and Tony—John is known in the industry as a fair, even-handed, and open-hearted collaborator.

"Every decision that you make, every personnel decision you make is critical in how you create art," he told us. As a vocal political activist and philanthropist, John looks for the right people, in the right context, at the right time in every project he undertakes. "In politics they say that personnel is policy. I would add that personnel is your art. Depending on whom you hire, you are going to get different energy. You're going to have different results from the people you surround yourself with. You're going to get different results in your cowriting. You want somebody you can rely on to be trustworthy on the business side but also creatively. You want people you can trust in the room. So choose wisely but also don't be afraid to experiment."

Pharrell's career is also a story of carefully choosing the right collaborators. At Adidas, at Chanel, or in the studio, Pharrell is acutely aware of finding the right coworkers.

"The most valuable thing in business are human beings," he told us. "Good ones are really hard to come by. And when you find them, you hold on to them. Everything else is material, right? That comes and goes but good people, not every day. So you want to surround yourself with people that you trust. So when challenges arise, your instincts and your reflexes tell you to listen to them."

Ask the founders of any start-up: the best collaborations are tied together by a shared vision and purpose, a commitment to shape a better future. If one person insists on his or her own way, then it's not a true collaboration; it's just another example of a bad boss and disgruntled employees. Far too often, in our role as business advisers, we meet executives who believe that ruthless competition is the foundation of good business and so pit one team against another or issue fiat directives about which department can work with (or even communicate with) others inside their own organization. Early in Michael's career, he was even asked by a client to visit the office only on Mondays or Fridays—times when other executives would be working offsite! This mentality clearly creates a culture of fear and leads to, among other things, bad products.

When John Lennon and Paul McCartney met as teenagers, it was their passion for rock music that brought them together. They would play hooky from school to spend the afternoons trading melodic and lyrical ideas, playing at being famous, mimicking their idols Elvis Presley and Buddy Holly. Their collaboration was legendary and met with unprecedented artistic and commercial success; even when they began songwriting independently, they still asked each other for help. They had widely divergent songwriting styles: Lennon was insecure and tempestuous, loose and less interested in the details, while McCartney would labor over every note. These differences made them a great team.

When George Harrison and Ringo Starr joined the band, they extended this flat hierarchy with a strict policy of "one man, one vote." But this did not remain true forever. Discord grew in the ranks, starting as a trickle. The rupture first became apparent when the band's manager, Brian Epstein, died unexpectedly. Many saw Epstein as the glue that held the band together, and the Fab Four began drifting apart, following their own interests. With Epstein gone, no one wanted to take over running the business side of their affairs. Artistically, McCartney wanted to continue in a pop music vein; Lennon drifted into avant garde explorations. Egos started getting in the way. Harrison and Starr were both writing songs, too, but they were unable to persuade Lennon or McCartney to record their music.

By the time the Beatles were in the studio for their ninth album, what had started as a trickle had grown to a torrent. Fans call it the *White Album* because of its plain white sleeve, but in later years McCartney referred to it as the "Tension Album." Lennon, McCartney, Harrison, and Starr had lost curiosity for one another. They no longer had a shared agenda.

There is a telling scene in the 1970 British film *Let It Be*, which documents the Beatles rehearsing and recording songs for their final studio album. In this scene, McCartney seems pushy and out of touch with what his bandmates want; Harrison stares at him, simultaneously bored and annoyed. Words are exchanged like blows. Not long after the film was shot, the band signed with a new manager, but McCartney refused to add his signature to the contract. At the time, the three other Beatles moved forward under the band's policy of "one man, one vote." But McCartney was strategic, even Machiavellian, in refusing to sign, aware that their personal code would not hold up in court. He was right: when he filed a lawsuit against his bandmates two years later, the court found in his favor. He was not contractually bound to remain with the Beatles. One man's vote outweighed the others, and one of the greatest collaborations in pop history came to a brutal end.

This is a familiar story of founders fighting founders: Jobs versus Wozniak at Apple, Eberhard versus Musk at Tesla, Zuckerberg versus Saverin at Facebook. In each case there is a loss of shared pursuit, a shift from "we, us, ours" to "I, me, mine."

This circumstance is, of course, not limited to founders. Leaders can find themselves at odds with their board, too. More often than not, a founder or CEO sees her mission differently than the

board does; when push comes to shove, the board sees her interpretation as risky to the stability of the business. That's how Jobs
got removed from Apple in the 1980s; Jack Dorsey was fired from
Twitter in 2008. On the bright side, despite these dramatic rejec-
tions, both Jobs and Dorsey eventually returned to lead the companies they cofounded because they were able to persuade their
boards that they had the vision to take their companies forward.

Even the Beatles eventually reunited, after a fashion, in 1995
to write a new song in support of the documentary *The Beatles
Anthology*. The song "Free as a Bird" was first demoed on a cassette
tape by John in 1977, while he was living in New York. When the
opportunity to contribute to the documentary arose, McCartney
asked Yoko Ono if any of Lennon's demos might work to develop
a new song. She shared a tape with the remaining band members, and they wrote an arrangement around John's posthumous
vocal melody. The song soared to the top of the charts, putting the
Beatles in the spotlight once again.

An Agile Approach

The company that operates more like a band of collaborators than
a strict corporate hierarchy has the ability to shape an environment
where everyone feels a sense of belonging. Equal parts freedom and
responsibility. We understand that it can be overwhelming to manage the many initiatives, agendas, and personalities that you deal
with on a daily basis—we've experienced this in our own careers.
Setting priorities as a team can be a challenge. Our defensive instincts, or desire just to stay sane, can overpower our curiosity, openness, and pursuit of others. In other words, they can destroy trust.

The good news is that in recent years, we have seen a growing
trend toward organizations that are structured to foster symbiotic
growth among employees. Agile companies are set up as a network of microteams to promote rapid learning and fast-moving
decision-making, enabled by technology and guided by a shared
common purpose. In a holacracy, like Zappos and Medium, the

org chart is deliberately flat. Rather than relying on a hierarchy of top-down direction, management and governance are decentralized and shared equally among stakeholders and employees; self-organizing teams share both purpose and objectives with equal autonomy and authority. The teal organizational model, devised by Belgium-born former McKinsey associate partner Frederic Laloux, intentionally pushes for a more soulful and engaged vision of leadership: mindful, taming the impulses of ego, and suspicious of the desire to control the environment, look good, or even do good in the world. By foregrounding each individual's personal journey and the value of humility, teal companies operate without an organizational chart or quarterly goals, opting instead for self-managed teams, intuitive reasoning, and distributed decision-making.

It's hard to say which model of collaborative business management is most effective; they all have their strengths. But each of them replaces Industrial Age ideas that no longer make sense in a dynamic twenty-first century—and they all come down to core questions: What does leadership look like today? How are decisions made? What model works best for your industry, your company, your project?

We asked Berklee's president, Roger Brown, to explain his own organizational philosophy. Since Roger took the helm seventeen years ago, the college has experienced incredible growth in enrollment and reach; before coming to Berklee, he was a high school teacher and founded a start-up focused on innovative childcare and early education. But for Roger, it all started with his experience as a drummer.

"When I think back on my relatively humble experience of being in bands—and I was in a ton of bands—they were all leaderless. We were four or five people, and we made decisions collectively. Different people played different roles. I tended to be the person who helped find gigs or helped get us organized."

When he cofounded his educational childcare provider Bright Horizons, he had no children and had not studied early childhood development. In fact, the only business experience he brought was two years of management consulting and two years of running a refugee program in Sudan.

"You could say there's a lot of hubris in thinking that you're the person who ought to start this organization," he said in his even-keeled, understated voice.

But he and his wife looked for the right team, key players with the knowledge to fill the gaps.

"We went out and hired an early childhood specialist from Tufts, who was fantastic," he told us. "We hired an operations person who had worked for a local childcare organization. We got a really good CFO. So our confidence was that we could find the right people to get the thing done, not confidence that we could somehow figure it all out by ourselves."

In developing the staff at Berklee, Roger has chosen people who are able to shift roles based on their knowledge and the priorities of serving students, likening his approach to forming a modern band.

"People like to say that running a business is like an orchestra, and you, as the leader, are the conductor of the orchestra. That's the 1950s model. You looked for someone who would play the part the way you wrote it. In the modern music model, you want a great sessions player who will come up with the part you never thought to write. Not ten people playing the same instrument, but a smaller team improvising in real time, observing and feeling what's coming from each other, really watching each other and working together. All without a score that someone wrote, either a year ago or two hundred years ago."

Roger believes in, and has demonstrated through his leadership, the effectiveness of a collaborative mindset. But he also knows that, with no single person directing everyone else, there must be an organizing principle that can guide strategy and decision-making—a clear idea of why your organization exists.

"Going away for six months and writing an orchestral piece, then rehearsing it for another six months before playing it—that model is one that doesn't take account of the way the world reacts to what you're doing. Instead, you observe, you try something, you listen, you amend it, you improvise," he said, drawing an analogy to strategic planning and operations. "I think the old model of how you did strategy was an arrogant one that assumed you were important, and the world cared about you. The new model is one of observing and sensing opportunity, looking at the current reality and asking: 'What is working well? How do we do more of that? What is not working well?'"

"I have a simple mantra, made up of two simple principles. First, I want to increase the attractiveness of Berklee to young people; second, I want to decrease the objections of their parents."

As we pointed out earlier, the misconceptions about musicians are broadly held. Roger explained that when a student is accepted at both a well-regarded Ivy League and Berklee, he has seen parents discourage attendance at Berklee because the value of a liberal arts music education isn't fully understood. His mission, his guiding light, as the college's president has been to make the value of a Berklee education clearer.

"I view everything I do through the lens of my two-part mantra. I test everything against it. If an idea doesn't work, then I quietly pass on it; if it is a perfect fit, we do it. Or, if it's close, we adapt it in some way, to make it more what we need."

This picture of how leadership can be collaborative—indeed, should be collaborative—is taking on new life through Berklee's City Music program. A twenty-five-year-old initiative, City Music started as an afterschool program when music programs were dropped from Boston public schools due to budget cuts. Primarily targeting students in underserved schools and neighborhoods,

City Music today touches the lives of students in fifty-two cities across North and South America.

The curriculum is designed to help middle and high school kids learn music by teaching music theory, instrument instruction, and ensemble through music they like, like chart-topping hits and scores from Pixar movies.

We asked David Mash, who oversaw global expansion of the program, for his thoughts on what makes a good leader and how the skills that music students learn translate to a business mindset. David is uniquely qualified to speak on the subject: he started out in the early 1970s as an artist-development representative for Motown Records and then played synthesizer with artists like Dave Brubeck as well as his own bands, before joining Berklee to found a program in music synthesis and eventually online learning.

"Of all the students we teach, less than 10 percent will become professional musicians," he told us. "But our goal is really youth development, through music. We prepare them for life. The discipline of studying music is similar to the discipline of studying anything; there's a strong connection between music and coding, between symbols and sound, symbols and meaning. There's an incredible self-satisfaction and self-esteem that comes with learning to make the sound you're looking for, and for some kids this is lacking in their other studies. But to me, the most important part is ensemble."

Thelonious Monk, a jazz piano icon and Miles Davis collaborator, once said: "All musicians are potential band leaders." This impulse is evident in City Music's approach to teaching collaboration.

"In any area of life, leadership boils down to how you get people to see your vision," David said. "If you're the guitar player in a band and you've written a piece that needs bass and drums and you have an idea in your head for how it should sound, you have to convince the players to hear it in their heads and pull it out of their fingers. You have to share that vision and inspire them to get excited about it. Learning to lead in that way prepares you for so much in the world."

The challenge for us as creative collaborators in any field is twofold: First, to be confident in our own skills so that other people can call on us to use them. Second, to be curious about the others so we can build amazing things together, with a shared vision and purpose.

Our night in the woods of Western Massachusetts is a good reminder that we all have a desire to create and connect with others. At its best, collaboration feels equally selfish and selfless, personally fulfilling and available to newcomers. Tourists created a community that lasted long after the last chime strike on the chapel. That night was an introduction to a new cohort of like-minded individuals, many of whom we've seen again every summer since.

When we are both confident in our abilities and curious about what others bring to the table—when both are firing on all cylinders—musicians and entrepreneurs discover a corollary benefit. Think of the dedication that people have to Apple, to Fender guitars, to Everlane, to a church or temple, even to a local community nonprofit. Organizations that are consistently open to working with others develop fans who share their purpose. "Wilco has been lucky to have the freedom to create," John Stirratt told us, "and I've been lucky to create outside of the field of music. It's an extended family."

A collaborative mindset, at its best and brightest, leads to just that: an extended family that provides mutual support, open communication, a sense of belonging, and the freedom that helps every member reach his or her creative goals.

Interlude 3

This playlist features supergroups, although we use that term loosely! Beyoncé's supergroup is her writing and production team, while the Traveling Wilburys are an iconic troupe of A-List troubadours who performed together: Bob Dylan, Roy Orbison, George Harrison, Jeff Lynne, and Tom Petty. Wilco has a steady lineup of accomplished musicians, each with his or her own side hustles. The Desert Sessions were recorded by a dream team from Autolux, Queens of the Stone Age, ZZ Top, and other bands during a long weekend in Palm Desert. Take a moment to read up on all of them.

HOLD UP, Beyoncé

GET LUCKY, Daft Punk, featuring Pharrell Williams and Nile Rodgers

BEWARE, Punjabi MC and Jay-Z

BEFORE YOUR VERY EYES, Atoms for Peace

RUSTY NAILS, Moderat

ALL CAPS, Madvillian

FEEL GOOD INC., Gorillaz

GET IT ON (BANG A GONG), Power Station

DON'T CALL HOME, Breeders

HANDLE WITH CARE, Traveling Wilburys

THE PAIN OF LOVING YOU, Trio

DAWNED ON ME, Wilco

NOSES IN ROSES, FOREVER, Desert Sessions

Deep Listening: *Give Up* by the Postal Service, an unexpected platinum-selling collaboration between Ben Gibbard of Death Cab for Cutie and Jimmy Tamborello, aka Dntel. The duo's name came from the process of mailing unfinished songs back and forth as they collaborated.

four
demoing

Get Dirty

Failure is something to be welcomed.

—Imogen Heap

On the eighth floor of Square's San Francisco headquarters, thirteen identical shadowboxes are tacked, without fanfare, to a blank wall. Inside each box is an iteration of the mobile payment company's credit card readers. The first and oldest is a rough and functional prototype, made of black plastic with exposed screw heads and a dirty loop of wire. As you walk down the row, the iterations become smaller and more refined, keeping what works and tossing what is unnecessary, until you arrive at the final frame holding the compact, bright white hardware of today, upon which the company's $6 billion valuation has been built. It's a beautiful picture of an idea taking shape, then being reshaped over and over again.

When a thought pops into the back of your mind, it is fluid, flexible, and indeterminate: Wouldn't it be great if people could use credit cards to pay each other as easily as they use cash? But the path to actualize an idea like this can seem daunting, the logistics overwhelming. What's the right first step?

Corporate innovation strategies often begin with an analysis of past failures or successes; we can't count how many times we've been asked to help make a company into "the Apple of toothpaste" or "the Uber of banking"! This approach is useful if you want to repeat history but is not so helpful for creating something that is truly new. Alternatively, companies might begin by brainstorming, bringing a concept to a group for interpretation and input. But brainstorms still require action.

At IDEO, the philosophy is that it's easier to know what you want to create once you start creating it. There's even a motto for this moment of doubt: "Don't get ready, get started." Sketch. Construct a mock-up. Even services can be visualized through storyboards and scale models, interactions and services through role playing. But get started by making something.

In business, this is called a prototype. In music, it's called a demo. In both cases, the creator's mindset is one of iteration. Every song that you have ever heard on the radio or streamed on your phone began as a humble demo. Musicians sit in studios or at kitchen tables and record the seed of a song. Musicians who are attuned to inspiration are constantly recording snippets of drumbeats or licks—and a lot of what they record never makes it onto an album. Rather than trying to decide where they want to end up, they make the abstract tangible by focusing on the feeling they want to express and sketching the skeleton of a song. A demo puts an idea to work.

Make It Dirty

By its nature, a demo is rough, sketchy, and messy. It is made quickly. Not only does this help prevent you from falling in love with the idea too soon, it delivers a prototype that is breakable and throwawayable. If a demo is treated as something precious, you might miss out on its shortcomings or, even worse, try to rush it to market. At this stage, perfection is not the goal; that would only close the door to further inspiration and creativity.

Michael Jackson's demos are a remarkable example. The controversy that surrounds Jackson's life and legacy is tragic and infuriating, yet we can acknowledge that he was a genius at songwriting. The demo that became his 1982 chart-topping "Billie Jean" is the song in its barest form: a simple progression of guitar chords, a drumbeat, only a hint of the famous synthesizer loop that became the backbone of the song. Jackson's commanding and wildly nimble voice sings a melody with very little of his trademark frills and flourishes. Many of the lyrics have not even been written yet, but he finds the notes. The song is far from finished, but his intention is crystal clear, and we can already see its promise, feel its heartbeat.

Sometimes a demo has a very different feel and a very different purpose. Dr. Susan Rogers is a professor of music production, engineering, and psychoacoustics at Berklee, but in the mid-1980s, she was lead sound engineer for the iconic pop artist Prince. A self-taught technician who never graduated from high school, Susan got the break of a lifetime when she landed a job at Prince's studios, where she worked during the peak of his commercial career and began collecting his studio and live recordings, which became the artist's famous vault of unreleased material.

"If Prince was awake, he was playing music. And if he was playing music, he was recording in some way," she told us. "He was the kind of thinker whose ideas came so fast, and he had so many, that he would carry a boom box around the house and hit record.

He'd just riff. Sometimes if we were at rehearsal and he was waiting for me to mic a drum, he would sit at the piano to capture
ideas. But they weren't demos per se. He had all the money in the
world, and all the lights on his highway were green."

In many ways, she said, he was his own producer and had carte
blanche. So the situation was different: Prince wasn't showing a
producer his vision for the song or bringing bandmates along on a
journey of discovery. It was all in his head, he just needed to capture his running stream of creativity on multitrack tape; Susan's
job was to record whatever was happening on the studio stage.
Prince, ever a polymath, played guitar, bass, piano, keyboard, synthesizer, clavinet, drums, and a wide variety of percussion instruments. Whether he was moving from instrument to instrument or
playing with a band, Susan took down every note so Prince could
later work out the details, integration, and arrangements. She told
us that the song "America," off his album *Girl*, was laid down entirely live with a band, recording in a single take, without stopping
for twenty-one minutes, until the tape ran out. That was the final
version. On the other hand, "Strange Relationship," released on
Sign o' the Times, required session after session over the course of
four years.

After he died, Prince's estate released *Originals*, fifteen of the
rumored thousands of demo songs that he had given to other performers ranging from Kenny Rogers ("You're My Love") to the
Bangles ("Manic Monday"). In many cases, Prince's demos are
more compelling—and, of course, funkier—than the other artists' versions. And in each one, Prince lays out his thoughts for
where the song could go. When *Originals* came out, drummer, DJ,
and Prince aficionado Questlove said that he was excited to hear
"what's under the hood."

A review in *Variety* called *Originals* the Purple One's best
and most accessible posthumous album, a cohesive and extremely
well-curated compilation that is perhaps most important because

of the insight it gives into his working methods and his imagination during the 1980s, when he was at the peak of his creative powers.

After Susan left Prince in the late 1980s, she went on to have a twenty-two-year career as a producer. Out of the rarefied air of Prince's studios, back in the world of mere mortals, demos are both different and the same.

"A demo is a prototype, showing the work you intend to do," Susan told us. "By nature, they are incomplete and unfinished, so a producer can hear the skeletal elements—melody, lyrics, rhythm, chord progression, maybe even harmony. It's not to show formal elements because we're going to redo those anyway, and it allows the producer to imagine the song with different rhythms or orchestration, even in a different key."

Her highest-grossing hit was the Barenaked Ladies' song "One Week." When she heard the song in skeletal form, Susan reimagined it to appeal to a wider audience.

"As a producer, you have to consider that you are the first follower," she said. "You are the first audience member, the first person to taste the soup as a chef is trying out a new recipe. You have to report back: it's too spicy, or the texture is weird. Next, it's the producer's job to consider how it could be optimized for the audience, taking your own taste into account, combining novelty and familiarity."

When she started working with the Barenaked Ladies, the band's audience tipped toward female at shows. So one of her aims was to pick up more males as fans. She led the band forward in slight changes to the lyrics and tone, very subtle things, and, as she put it, "a hell of a lot of guesswork."

As it turns out, Susan's guesses were gold, as was the album she helped create. Her work on the Barenaked Ladies' album and, in particular, its megahit "One Week," enabled Susan to pay off her mortgage and, at the age of forty-four, fulfill a lifelong dream of enrolling in college. And she didn't stop schooling until she achieved a PhD in music cognition.

"Both engineering and the sciences are the domains of systems thinkers, people who are really interested in how the knee bone connects to the shin bone to the ankle bone," she said. "Starting with a seed of an idea, you have to think through how all of the parts come together. A friend of mine, the sculptor Tim Buckner, said that a life in the arts is a life of problem solving. It's true in music, and in the business side of music, and in entrepreneurship too. You can go your whole career never having seen all of the possible problems, as many and diverse as life itself."

Even though Prince's first recordings of songs were more polished than most, demos often have a raw intimacy and visceral authenticity. They are in some ways the purest form of a song because they are closest to the moment of inspiration. So it's no surprise that in the 1990s, a decade of reaction to the glittery excesses of the '80s, this rawness and grit became a kind of artistic ideal. Low-fidelity DIY recordings of bands like Beat Happening, Bikini Kill, Sparklehorse, Pavement, Smog, and Nirvana took the sincerity of the demo as their ultimate aim. Rather than creating flawless productions, these bands wanted a song to be technically rudimentary and very close to its intent and meaning. The final versions released on their albums stay remarkably close to the spirit of the original.

Austin-based songwriter Daniel Johnston was an early inspiration for many of these bands. He was a pioneer in the lo-fi music scene, whose deliberately crude and deeply personal recordings rejected the heavily produced popular music of the day. Resisting both commercialism and cynicism, Johnston's albums maintain a childlike simplicity, the feeling of an outsider artist or naïve genius; he sings straightforward lyrics in a wobbly voice, cool but earnest, heartbreaking and hilarious at the same time. For most of his life, Johnston recorded songs in obscurity, passing out demo tapes while working at McDonald's, until Kurt Cobain went to the MTV Video Music Awards wearing a T-shirt with cover art from Daniel Johnston's "Hi, How Are You?" tape cassette released nine years earlier. Suddenly propelled to cult stardom, his music was covered in the years following by the Flaming Lips, Death Cab for Cutie, Bright Eyes, and Beck.

Johnston's recordings felt familiar to artists who had always made demos, but they also seemed like an entirely new way to make music. "There's so much potential in his songs, but it's rarely fully realized, and that's kind of the beauty of it," said Jeff Tweedy of Wilco. "For a songwriter like myself, hearing the music in such a raw state is exciting. There's so much to draw you in. You can get lost in the potential, in how much he leaves open to interpretation."

In 2019, Tweedy announced *Chicago 2017*, a live album recorded with Johnston during his final performance in the Windy City, before Johnston died of a heart attack at the age of fifty-eight. Proceeds from the album benefited the Hi, How Are You Project, a nonprofit started by Daniel and his family to inspire conversation around mental health issues. In a statement, Tweedy said: "There is and was only one Daniel, and to be able to work with him and help present his music was a huge honor for me and the band, one for which we are all very thankful."

In 2014, Tweedy told the *Atlantic* that Johnston inspired emotional honesty and a raw, visceral quality of recordings. "I've thought about Johnston a lot in my own work with words and lyrics," he said. "Lyrics are a very tricky thing to write, because songs, in my mind, are ruled by melody. I really believe that melody does all the heavy lifting emotionally. When I write lyrics, or when I adapt a poem to a song, what I really want to do is not interfere with the spell that's being cast by the melody. Basically, I just don't want to fuck it up. I just want to stay out of the way. At the same time, I hope—at best—that the words enhance some meaning or clarify somehow what the melody makes me feel."

Tweedy's own songwriting process places incredible weight on the demo as a building block. For each new song, he records a first pass that is little more than melodic gibberish sung to chords strummed on a guitar and then repeatedly listens to his own demo, obsessively reworking what he hears from different angles. On an episode of the podcast *Song Exploder*, he breaks down how he works:

"I'll do a vocal melody based just on sounds. We call them 'mumble tracks.' And I will sit and listen to the first line over and over, and sketch things on my notepad, and try to figure out [lyrics] that have the same syllables, the same meter, until I get something that's satisfying. And then I'll sing it."

In his biography *Let's Go (So We Can Get Back)*, Tweedy explains further: "I'm drawn to this approach to writing lyrics because it keeps me attached to a song in its early state, the way it was before I'd thought it through and figured out what it was. I don't feel like I'm always trusted to make the best choices consciously. I trust myself enough to commit to a process, see what gets made, and respond with feeling and intuition."

As the lyrics come together, they have an impact and smoothness that are exhilarating, words that at first might sound random but unpack a deeper meaning in the greater context of the narrative.

Tweedy passes the demo to his bandmates once he's satisfied—but before the song is anywhere near completion, while it still feels like an opportunity for discovery rather than something fully defined and determined. There's a great lesson here for collaborators: it's not enough to tell partners or teammates an idea; you have to help them see, hear, and feel what you are thinking, in ways that still leave space for them to cocreate. John Stirratt, the Wilco bassist who founded Tourists hotel we mentioned earlier, told us that when a demo is ready the band continues this process as they write music for their own instruments.

"When we receive a demo of the acoustic and vocal, we simply imagine a framework that our instruments would provide for the tune. And much of the fun comes from how these parts might work with what the other musicians had imagined."

Again, the key is to keep it quick and dirty.

Can I Ask Me a Question?

When roughing out a prototype or recording a demo, it's also helpful to ask yourself why you are creating it. This gives your idea focus and allows you to iterate on the question behind the idea as you improve on each subsequent version.

Jeff Tweedy's son Spencer, at the age of twenty-five, is already a talented drummer who has recorded with Mavis Staples and Norah Jones. He is also an entrepreneur, helming a start-up company called Fjord Audio, which manufactures accessories for recording studios. Not long ago, we were browsing through *Tape Op*, a magazine dedicated to creative recording techniques, when we came across an interview where he said: "To me, anything that you do that requires problem solving or thinking through a lot of alternatives can be called design. . . . The most exciting projects to me are the ones that incorporate unconscious thinking with superconscious tinkering."

A musician talking about design? When we read this, we nearly fell out of our seats! We got in touch with him and asked him to tell us more about the idea of tinkering, which in our view is a wonderful word to describe how artists and entrepreneurs alike build on a demo. Tall with mussed brown hair, Spencer has his father's shy smile when he talks. His speech picks up tempo when he's following a train of thought.

"I think there's a parallel process between writing a song and designing a project," he told us. "Both start with one bit of inspiration, pretty much completely unconscious, and then move into a more iterative, more conscious process of allowing yourself to edit. You can't do the same chord patterns next to each other too repetitively. You bring in all of your prior experience of how songs ought to be arranged."

Spencer applied this same approach in founding Fjord Audio. He told us that he never set out to become an entrepreneur; he simply had an appreciation for products that most people would consider to be disposable commodities but which were manufactured with real care and attention to detail. His time in studios gave him the bug to contribute something to that environment. So he started looking for electric and audio component parts online and then hired a friend, Johnny Balmer of Alchemy Audio in Chicago, to solder test models.

A breakthrough moment happened when he was at his parents' home. "I saw an extension cord made by Conway Electric. Conway is an amazing company based in California that uses old circular looms to make cotton covers for their extension cords. They're beautiful. And I asked myself: 'Why isn't there anything that looks this good for recording studios? I wonder if I could apply that same look to cables?' So I contacted Conway on Instagram to ask if they could produce cotton cable jackets for audio. The owner, Kevin Faul, replied almost immediately: 'How many feet do you need?'"

As we got to know Spencer, we were delighted by his humility and thoughtfulness. At one point in our dialogue, he stepped back and said: "There were moments when I thought about scrapping the project because making an accessory seemed so inconsequential. But I felt that it'd be worthwhile to understand what it's like to make a product, however small run and small need it turned out to be."

This idea challenged his personal convictions about products and process, commodities and creativity.

"I have the attitude—which I think is the default in American and Western culture—that once a product is 'finished' and its components are locked, that it has a static identity. It becomes a form, and every individual unit that gets produced is just a manifestation of that form. It seems freaky that this mindset glosses over the individuality and uniqueness of each individual unit, even if it's virtually indistinguishable from the next one. It seems to put all of the weight and meaning of a product on the abstract side. Whereas when it comes to writing music, I really like to put the meaning on the process side. The experience of making something. I learned that from my dad: that the most important part of making something is in the process, in losing yourself in creativity, rather than in being able to look back later on an artifact."

Taking a songwriter's approach to both process and product, he spent more than a year prototyping iterations of Fjord cables.

"I learned three main things from the test units. First was that we had to get the weight right; the first base cable I picked felt too thin, so I wound up using the normal profile version. Second, Conway had developed a lacquering technique to give their cotton covers better grip and keep them from getting dirty, but I thought it made the cables harder to coil, so we had to come up with a better solution. Third, even though Johnny is a superskilled solderer and technician, some of the solder points inside the connectors broke during use. So we decided to use heat-shrink tubing over the solder points in future assemblies."

At every phase of development, Spencer returned to his original question: Can we create an accessory product that is well made and beautiful? This meant keeping prices reasonable and required him to let go of ideas that were cost prohibitive.

"At the time, I was really into the idea that the cables would arrive in custom packaging that doubles as a reusable holder. I prototyped a design out of cardboard and contacted molded paper pulp suppliers, but the cost of molds was too high." He even took a DIY approach to investment. "I was wary of doing a Kickstarter campaign because I hated the idea of asking my friends and family for money but eventually decided to view it as another extension of the creativity of the project. That I'd learn a lot from designing the campaign page, making a campaign video. So I borrowed my mom's camera and took product photos of test cables in six colorways. The connectors weren't even soldered on yet, they were just pushed over the cable!"

Iterating Is Testing

Charles and Bernice "Ray" Eames were two of the most influential American designers in the twentieth century. Working primarily in architecture and furniture design, the couple followed the modernist style but also pushed back against the heavy-handedness of many modernists by introducing simple elegance and a hint of whimsy. Their office created some of the most iconic pieces in the history of furniture: tall and cheerful stools with steep legs, beautiful lounges with plush leather seats, perfectly crafted chairs made of bent plywood.

The Eames Office was also known for extensive and meticulous prototyping throughout the design phase of product development, a practice learned from Finnish modernist Eero Saarinen. Saarinen frequently broke a design concept down into its essential elements—often dozens—then methodically proceeded to make dozens more studies of each piece. It's a fascinating approach and has applications far beyond product design: to discover how to develop a concept, break it down into its smallest parts, whether that is an individual component of a system, a desired outcome, or a series of notes. When each part has been isolated, you're ready to explore how it can be manipulated or changed. Each element becomes a prototype with its own question to be tested; each success or failure becomes an answer. It should include an element of what you believe is true.

In October 2017, along with other partners from IDEO, Michael took a bus from San Francisco to Sonoma County to visit the home of the Eames's granddaughter Llisa Eames Demetrios. Since Ray Eames died in 1988, Llisa has collected and catalogued artifacts from the Eames Studio, loaning pieces to museums around the world. She showed us a vast collection of furniture prototypes: version upon version of fiberglass chairs, molded plywood forms, and scale models, each one easily identifiable as predecessors to the Eames canon. Among the most fascinating was

a long room in the annex of a barn where tables were neatly pep-
pered with scores of joints and fasteners—discrete components
that go unnoticed, since they are mounted to the underside of the
furniture. Minute changes from one to another showed how the
designers advanced each idea as materials and manufacturing capabilities changed: bread crumbs that chart the evolving DNA of
the Eames portfolio.

Back in the house, we sat with Llisa in her living room. She
had recently converted old reel-to-reel tapes of a series of lectures
given by her grandfather to digital audio and wanted us to hear
them. The lectures were delivered during his appointment to the
Charles Eliot Norton Professorship of Poetry in 1971; it might
seem odd that an architect and designer would be tapped for a
poetry fellowship, but Harvard uses the term in its broadest sense,
celebrating the art of making ideas tangible. It was striking to hear
Charles share his ideas, to hear the thoughtful cadence of his voice
bringing them to life.

At one point, during a question-and-answer session, he was
asked how his studio has won so many awards. Rather than brush-
ing the question aside or letting it stroke his ego, he demystified
his process by recalling a collaboration with Saarinen:

"This is the trick. I give it to you; you can use it. We looked at
the program and divided it into all the essential elements—which
turned out to be about thirty-some-odd elements—and we proceeded methodically to make a hundred studies of each element,"
he said. "And we made one hundred studies of all combinations
of these elements, trying to not erode the quality that we had
gained. . . . And took these elements and began to then search for
the logical combinations of the combinations."

Imagine the mathematics of this: To find the ideal ratio between a curved piece of wood and a thin metal chair leg, for example, the Eames Studio explored three thousand options and then
added one hundred studies of combinations of the best ones. It

might be easy to dismiss his statement as hyperbole, but the artifacts in Llisa's barn backed it up.

When you are tinkering, consider breaking an idea down into its essential parts, but remember that parts cannot only be considered on their own; they must be seen in the context of the whole. By choosing the most promising combination of the most promising elements, you arrive at the bare minimum—a whole new starting point. What set the Eames Office apart was their willingness to toy with every particular during the prototyping phase. At some point, you have to make the choice to proceed, to believe that you've got it right. But the longer you play with every contingency, and the more patience you have for the experiment, the closer to perfect your final product will be.

Failing Is Fleeting

After working for five months to create the first-ever nickel-iron battery, Thomas Edison reportedly quipped: "I have not failed, not once. I've discovered ten thousand ways that don't work." Edison might be playing with semantics, but he understood that failure is built into the process of iteration. As many books and articles have pointed out, for many corporations, failure is still anathema, but artists know that it is actually an asset to creativity.

Songwriting, like business innovation, is a process of incremental iteration. As an artist studies a simple phrase or chord progression, he takes the many small steps of progressive development, rather than rushing toward completion. In business, approaching a plan or even a pitch is one way, much like a demo, of coming up with the raw goods to simulate what your product or service will look like. The process of working through a number of models, trying a variety of approaches, and drawing from the best of each one meets reality when you test your idea.

Musicians are also familiar with stumbles, failures, and rejection. After all, music is a rejection industry: you reject your own ideas as not quite right, your album is rejected by labels, your set is rejected by audiences. And you either give up, or you tweak it and try again. It's humbling but also strengthening. At the very least, failure exposes your assumptions and demonstrates relevance; but at its best, it produces something that gets people's feet tapping.

When Radiohead's *OK Computer* was released in 1997, it was a groundbreaking accomplishment that changed rock music. Combining labyrinthine guitar work, orchestral arrangements, intricate digital production techniques, and challenging song structures, the album was at once a commentary on the consumerism and materialism of the decade, a chilling prophecy of twenty-first-century technology-infused living, and an intimate confessional. The album was at the top of nearly every list that year, and the band members became reluctant rock art icons.

To Radiohead fans, one of the most striking things was how different *OK Computer* is from the band's previous albums. Their first, *Pablo Honey*, produced a massive hit in "Creep," which had a sardonic darkness that set the band apart—but on the whole the album was the debut of a masterfully off-beat alternative group that sat awkwardly as a British counterpart to Nirvana, Pearl Jam, Soundgarden, and other bands in the rising grunge rock scene. *The Bends*, Radiohead's sophomore release, was more mature, full of beautiful and skillfully composed songs, but was still fairly straightforward guitar rock. So where did *OK Computer*'s new sound come from? Hours and hours of iteration, testing, and failures. The band had seen enough success with their first two offerings that their label gave them creative control and allowed them to set up a kind of laboratory—perhaps better described as a playroom. According to band leader Thom Yorke, setting up "weird spaces" was not only a critical part of the process but one of the things that he loves doing most.

The Cure had just wrapped recording of their album *Wish* in actress Jane Seymour's manor house, a fourteen-acre retreat in

Southern England. Radiohead moved in with all of their equipment and brought an engineer-cum-producer, Nigel Godrich, who had contributed to the more experimental songs on *The Bends*. In two three-week sessions, they played with ideas and sounds.

"The big thing is we didn't want to go into conventional recording studios," guitarist Ed O'Brien told *Rolling Stone*. "We felt that there was this whole move to make the space our own."

To the band, it felt like the adults were away on vacation, and they could work without any restrictions. Cables criss-crossed the property. While working on a song, they would move from room to room, testing the acoustics. The ballroom had a wooden floor and paneling on the walls, as well as a large medieval tapestry, which created a beautiful sound in the room. The library's book-lined shelves and a nursery full of soft plush toys created more muted acoustics. Out back was an ornamental greenhouse, where Yorke recorded vocals for the song "Paranoid Android," surrounded by glass.

But the experiments went beyond the sound of spaces. A buzzing sound on "Karma Police" was sampled from a humming refrigerator. Yorke recorded snippets of dialogue from the film *Three Days of the Condor*, off a television set. The drums on "Airbag," the album's first track, were inspired by DJ Shadow, a departure for the band: Godrich asked Thom to create a loop, and he went to a room with dead sound to mix it until he was ready to bring it back to guitarist Jonny Greenwood—who ran the track through effects pedals. In the end, they didn't use everything, but they kept three tracks of distortion and other effects. The band let themselves follow whatever tangent took their interest, any idea that popped into their heads or caught their ears, just to see where it might lead. They were, to use Spencer Tweedy's word, tinkering.

Twenty years after *OK Computer* was initially released, Radiohead put out a direct-to-fans box set edition of the album that included Yorke's handwritten journals from the sessions as well as a ninety-minute mixtape of unreleased demos and sonic experiments. Then a hacker stole a hard drive containing eighteen more hours of recordings from Yorke and circulated a threat of releasing them on the internet unless the band paid a ransom of $150,000. Instead, Radiohead decided to release the recordings themselves, with sales benefiting the environmental nonprofit Extinction Rebellion. Taken together, *OK Computer*'s experiments-in-the-raw paint a picture of the unbridled curiosity, willingness to risk failure, and commitment to iterate repeatedly until the band was satisfied.

Listening to this supplemental material, it is apparent that *OK Computer* could easily have become a reprise of *The Bends*. Several songs on the B side, including "Lift" and "Palo Alto," have song structures and poppy hooks similar to what the band had done before. And there are a surprising number of live recordings of "Airbag" that sound like a 1960s psychedelic jam band zoning out to ten-minute Hammond organ solos as they worked out the songs in public. But the recorded hours of sonic play give clues of how Radiohead arrived at their new sound. Not all of the explorations worked, especially the organ jams, and not all of the explorations on these tracks are obviously related to individual songs or even to the album's overall aesthetic. But we can connect the dots on some tracks: the supplemental sonic experiment "ZX Spectrum," for example, is a rich series of modular, layered synthesizer arpeggios, a harmonized chorus of digital blips and bleeps—a far cry from the guitar-driven path that had brought the band fame. Yet the track appears at the end of the *OK Computer* song "Let Down" as a sparkling texture.

Perhaps Edison was right: nothing is a failure. Or, to put it another way: no apparent failure should be discarded. Every prototyping test that pushes into something new is valuable. When you are building on a demo, iterating and testing, remember Radiohead's eighteen hours of play. Many of the sounds they explored during these sessions only later found the context where they truly fit on later albums. One song, aptly named "True Love Waits," was not finished and released until twenty years later.

Everything Is a Beta

In our digital world, beta testing has become the norm. Pop-up restaurants, single-season shops, small-scale festivals—all of these work in the same manner as a music demo. Most of the technology products we use on a regular basis are in permanent beta mode, constantly being iterated with new updates based on customer feedback. Get the spirit of the idea, build upon it, try it out with audiences, and learn firsthand from the obstacles and opportunities.

It is entirely appropriate to think of everything that Apple has done, from the introduction of the first iPod to the most recent iPhone, as a single continuous stream of demoing and development. Consider the lowly "home" button. The first iPod, released in 2001, shocked users with its touch-sensitive wheel for scrolling. While its appearance may have been inspired by the Braun transistor radio, Apple designers took the idea much further when they realized that every function of a music player could be carried out using a wheel and the keys that surround it. With every new version of the iPod, the wheel and button became more streamlined. The first-generation iPhone kept the button, although the wheel had been replaced by a full touchscreen. A few years later, in its continuing quest to remove mediating technology from the user experience, Apple left the home button behind. After all, Steve Jobs's goal had always been for the device to be usable with only a finger, the most natural human-to-machine interface. This always-beta mindset is also operative at Uber, Facebook, Twitter, Airbnb, and many other tech giants. The thirteen prototypes on the wall at Square don't even include the dozens of other sketches that were explored, including an acorn-shaped version inspired by the company's original name: Squirrel.

At each of these companies, there has never been a "final version" of an app or service on offer. Each iteration is built upon the prior version and serves as a foundation for the next. Panos's own start-up, Sonicbids, started with a niche need and iterated until it grew into a one-of-a-kind global platform. He started his career as a talent agent, working with artists like Nina Simone, Pat Metheny, Chick Corea, and Leonard Cohen, but he also met with talented musicians who were just starting their careers and struggling to book gigs. When he called music promoters to pitch them, there was no way to share their music quickly and easily. This was in 2001, before digital downloads, before YouTube or SoundCloud had been founded, so he would describe their sound over the telephone and promise to drop a CD in the mail. As you can imagine, Panos spent wild amounts of money shipping these CDs and was at the same time bombarded with mail from musicians who were looking to connect with bookings. Eventually, he found himself telling young artists that he couldn't take them on unless they could command $3,000 or more a night. The math simply didn't add up, and it was heartbreaking. He knew there had to be a better way to bring rising talent together with promoters on a shared platform.

So he created one. Sonicbids is an online marketplace that enables any band to go online and create a profile including a bio, photos, awards, and a history of shows they've played before—a shift to online marketing that helped redefine how bands connect with opportunities and audiences.

Sonicbids's first iteration was an early beta, literally built at the kitchen table and funded with Panos's personal credit cards and friends' and family's money since no bank would give him a merchant account without physical goods as collateral (think how much has changed in twenty years!). But he still faced a major challenge in how to get the right players to the table. It was a classic chicken and egg problem: Which comes first, artists or promoters? So he packed a bag with plenty of marketing material, went to the South by Southwest (SXSW) Music Festival in Texas, and leaned into his skills as a former talent agent. At meetings with promoters, he proposed a deal: if they put a listing on Sonicbids, he would pay for the first five bands they booked. Five paid gigs? An easy choice for a promoter.

Suddenly his beta took off. Live connections were happening every day. By 2013, when the company was acquired in a deal backed by Guggenheim Partners and subsequently became part of its Billboard Music Group, Sonicbids was the de facto standard for bands to connect with music promoters around the world. The platform had more than 500,000 bands and 35,000 promoters as members, and more than one million shows had been booked in one hundred countries. It had built exclusive partnerships with Austin's SXSW, Bonnaroo Music and Arts Festival, Seattle's Bumbershoot Music Festival, New York's CMJ, Milwaukee's Music Fest, and many others and had helped artists like the Lumineers, Temper Trap, Macklemore, and Arcade Fire get their first gigs.

It all started with a demo, a prototype, a beta.

Who Gon' Stop Me

Kanye West, the American rapper, singer, producer, and entrepreneur, gave new meaning to the idea that a beta is never finished when he was developing *The Life of Pablo*, one of his most celebrated albums. Over the course of several weeks, he created three unique versions of the album, one after another. His flexibility with his vision for the album, almost to the moment of its release, is an amazing window into his artistic process.

He knew that he wanted to transform his image by promising an album of "gospel rap," "a living, breathing, changing artistic expression" that was more positive and emotional than his earlier records. But the specifics were negotiable, iterable. In the months leading up to the launch of the first version, Kanye teased his audience with snippets of the songs on social media. Fans knew that some of the material would be discarded, and it became a kind of sport to guess which ones would make the final cut. He also used Twitter to workshop titles for the album, asking his fans for feedback: *So Help Me God*, *SWISH*, and *Waves* were runners-up to *The Life of Pablo*.

Of the many things that can be said about Kanye, no one can claim that he needs a hype man. After publicly testing different ideas for the record, he played the first version in its entirety at Madison Square Garden, during the launch of his clothing line Yeezy 3. The next morning, Kanye was back in the studio with only three days to deliver a second iteration, which he had promised exclusively to streaming service Tidal. Tidal is owned by his friend Jay-Z, and Kanye at the time owned a large stake in the company. So he switched out songs, changed lyrics, and made significant production changes. The version on Tidal sounded different, felt different. Fans took notice, and it became the first-ever streaming-only album to go platinum.

But Kanye still wasn't finished. As his audiences watched, delighted, he went back to the studio and made still more changes for general release. *The Life of Pablo* received five Grammy nominations and, following Tidal's release to competing streaming services, debuted at number one on the US Billboard 200.

On the cover of *The Life of Pablo* are the words *which/one*. Kanye knew that a big part of the album's appeal was that it had no definitive, final form. After all, in music there are few rights and wrongs. There is no final product. Think of bands that play one of their hits year after year, decade after decade. At every concert, they recreate it anew. Every song ever recorded is waiting to be covered by another band or sampled for a remix.

This is more than a valuable lesson for entrepreneurs; it is a way of thinking and moving through the world. How boring it is to believe that an original idea, posed as a question, has only one answer. It's much more inspiring and fun to know that we can always find improvements, that unexpected obstacles and possibilities to be explored are just around the corner. The company that tries to fight change is swimming upstream against reality, which is often messy, always in process, and indescribably beautiful. We thrive when we know that when it comes to prototyping, demoing, iterating, and testing, there is no finish line.

Interlude 4

From the stripped-down strumming of John Lennon to the pitch-perfect arrangements of Prince, the rough yet polished first drafts by Michael Jackson, and the surprising iterations by Bruce Springsteen, these demos show how artists communicate their intention with demos. One standout here is the "mumble tracks" sung by David Byrne on "Dancing for Money."

STRAWBERRY FIELDS DEMO, Beatles

BEAT IT DEMO, Michael Jackson

LET'S DANCE DEMO, David Bowie

DANCING FOR MONEY (UNFINISHED OUTTAKE),
    Talking Heads

REHAB DEMO, Amy Winehouse

BORN IN THE USA DEMO, Bruce Springsteen

ALL APOLOGIES DEMO, Nirvana

SHE'S A JAR DEMO, Wilco

WALTZ #1 DEMO, Elliot Smith

MANIC MONDAY DEMO, Prince

GEEZER LOVE, Spencer Tweedy

Deep Listening: Sometimes artists like the demos so much that they release them as finished albums. Check out *Nebraska* by Bruce Springsteen, an intimate album recorded in two days at home on his personal four-track tape recorder, and *Untitled Unmastered* by Kendrick Lamar, featuring songs recorded during the *To Pimp a Butterfly* sessions.

five
producing

Bring the Best Out in Others

I don't care what anybody plays, I just care who's playing it. I want that person to put all of his love and his whole self, his whole heart, into what he's doing.

—T Bone Burnett

In the preceding chapters, we have been highlighting the mindsets that bring musicians' ideas to life, but there is an adjacent mindset, one that helps others achieve their vision or reach their creative heights. While the word *producer* has grown in popularity due to hip-hop, it has become familiar in our pop-culture subconscious for decades because of movies. What does the word *producer* actually mean? If you sit through the end credits of any movie, you'll often see a laundry list of producers, whose functions range from financing to serving as bridges between multiple production companies to planning the actual process of filming. Independent films tend to have more producers than Hollywood movies; to date, Lee Daniels's *The Butler* holds the record with five producers, seventeen executive producers, six coexecutive producers, four coproducers, and seven associate producers!

In the music industry, the role of producer is a bit different. In the last decade it's been associated with highly collaborative beat makers like Timbaland, Diplo, Pharrell, and Drake. A more classic embodiment of the role is analogous to a film director: the person who oversees all aspects of the creation of a work of art.

Some producers have notoriously ruled their artists with an iron fist, directing recording sessions, selecting which songs to record, and choosing which licks and loops make the final cut. Their fingerprints can be seen on every detail. There are legendary stories of dictator-producers, relentlessly committed to their own vision for a song or album. Rock and Roll Hall of Famer Phil Spector demanded absolute creative control over every recording, even when he worked with incredible talent like the Righteous Brothers ("You've Lost That Lovin' Feelin'"), the Ramones (*End of the Century*), and John Lennon ("Imagine"). He was known for bullying artists to achieve his idea of musical perfection, waving guns and tossing musicians out of his studio so he could complete a song without their input. He was so tyrannical that he eventually lost control and murdered an actress who rejected his advances, putting him in prison for nineteen years to life. Clearly, not a role model.

But his style of managing (sans the pistol) might sound familiar if you have ever worked in a dysfunctional organization where command-and-control, "my way or the highway" leadership is encouraged. Thankfully, such companies are less common today (or have failed). As the world of business has changed to a virtual, global marketplace that is always on and staffed by multiple generations with varying values, leadership has become more agile. While still decisive, executives and managers understand the importance of empowering rather than controlling, leading from a place of trust by exploring and building upon the motivations of people who work with them.

In the music industry, a more agile approach has also proven to be extremely effective. Producers like Hank Shocklee, T Bone Burnett, and Jimmy Iovine have seen incredible success working as mentor, consultant, and coach to musicians, helping the artists develop their own vision, grow in new ways, and share their creations with the world. Seeing all of the variables at any given moment, then nipping, tucking, pruning, grafting, molding, and sculpting that moment into its best form. In this chapter, we're going to look at the three producers above, as well as American businessman and entrepreneur Steve Stoute, drawing out lessons on how to get the best work from yourself and the people you work with, rather than simply demanding conformity to a plan.

Make the Best Thing for You, Then Share It

Hank Shocklee is a founding member of the American hip-hop group Public Enemy and production team the Bomb Squad. Hank has worked with Rick Rubin and Russell Simmons at Def Jam Records; produced albums for LL Cool J, Bell Biv DeVoe, and EPMD; and remixed albums for Peter Gabriel and Sinéad O'Connor. When we asked Hank about how he works in the studio, he zoomed immediately out to the big picture.

"If you look at all of the matter in the universe, it only equates to about 3 percent of all known energy," Hank told us. "So there's 97 percent of nothingness, what we call space, and in that space is an infinite amount of energy. We don't know much about it because we're not taught to deal with that. Why do we think of it as nothingness? Does matter define the space, or does space define the matter? To me, the larger is always the thing that describes the smaller. And that space is what I want to tap into. I want to let that energy direct all projects in everything that I'm doing."

This might sound esoteric, but Hank has made an art of putting this idea into practice. During his days at Def Jam, the label signed Slick Rick, a Bronx rapper with a reputation for bringing strong and controversial opinions to the studio. Slick Rick butted heads with the label; none of their lead producers—Rubin, Simmons, and Larry Smith—could make it work. After more than a year of efforts, Hank says he stepped in with a different approach, one that reflects his desire to tap into the 97 percent that is unknown. The resulting album, *The Great Adventures of Slick Rick*, climbed to number one on the Billboard hip-hop chart and went platinum, with over a million sales.

"What I decided was that I could shape his record without halting or hindering his creative mindset, what he wanted to get across," he told us. "Rick has strong ideas. He knows exactly what he wants to get done. So instead of me leading the project, I told him I was going to follow. I was his assistant, and that's what made the project work. It's his best record because I allowed him to be him. Rather than managing the person, I managed the environment around him."

In a very real way, a great producer is nearly absent, or invisible, because his work is all about the artist, creating space for her to succeed. Hank's taste is influential, and his experience is invaluable, but his focus is on the person and the project—sitting with the artist, listening to her, removing obstacles or self-doubt that might get in the way, so she can tune into her own inspiration, helping her explore ways to grow and do her best work.

As Hank talked, we felt a deep resonance with his words, based on what we have felt so many times in our own work. The best outcomes from teams are not due to our own heavy-handed actions; instead, we succeed best when we succeed together. This is far from a platitude: it's an essential lesson in leadership, in the craft of creating the right conditions for other people to thrive. It's culture building, mentoring, and—as Hank says—helping. And it's especially true if you are lucky enough to have a team of superstars, accomplished people with ambition and energy. The last thing they need is to feel that they are in someone else's hands. You want the people you lead to know they have been set up for success.

When Michael first rose to leadership positions, rather than modeling his management style upon his band experiences, he modeled it after the professional leaders he worked under, which unfortunately did not include the behaviors Hank described. Instead, he perpetuated the same abuses of authority that had been applied to him: making people work late to show their loyalty to the organization; criticizing their ideas because he believed that, as the boss, his ideas were better; seeing employees as a means to an end rather than creative collaborators; and even taking credit for work because he was higher on the org chart.

It took Michael years to unlearn these behaviors. Even his first year at IDEO, in 2008, had a rough start. But a genuinely concerned colleague flagged a team interaction that created a moment of clarity: Michael stepped into a project room and briefly critiqued what he saw and then left due to a tight schedule. There's a name for this leadership behavior in the creative industry: "poop and swoop," like a bird dive-bombing then flying away! The project leader followed Michael down the hallway, asked him to sit down, and then said, "Dude, that was uncool. You didn't ask any questions. You had no idea where the team was in the project or what they wanted your feedback on. It totally demoralized everyone. You can't do this here." His words hit Michael like a ton of bricks. He realized that he had blown it and immediately went back to the team to apologize. In his past jobs, this is how the boss acted, but in this new role, leadership was not a command-and-control proposition.

Through interactions like this, and thanks to great mentors, Michael learned that the best creative environments are ones in which people are cared for, not ones where everyone is trying to live up to the expectations of a mad and passive-aggressive creative authoritarian. He began modeling himself with new principles: asking questions more than giving answers, ensuring designers were taking care of themselves, helping colleagues pursue interests that fed their creativity and strengthened their art. He began seeing associates as people first because in a business environment dignity can easily be taken away by making people solutions to your own problems rather than collaborators to address the challenges at hand. He began to understand himself as the manager of the culture, not the people. Not only can this unlock deeper creative growth in the workplace, it is also a better way of working for us as leaders.

Look for Their First Love, and Share It Wholeheartedly

T Bone Burnett is an American musician, songwriter, and producer who first found fame as a guitarist in Bob Dylan's band in the 1970s. He has gone on to become an Oscar-winning songwriter and (thirteen-time) Grammy Award–winning producer, working with artists who include Alison Krauss and Robert Plant, Counting Crows, Elvis Costello, Gillian Welch, Gregg Allman, John Mellencamp, Los Lobos, and Roy Orbison, as well as for composing film scores, including the films *Cold Mountain*, *Crazy Heart*, *O Brother, Where Art Thou?*, and the Johnny Cash biopic *Walk the Line*. In May 2020, we asked him about management, leadership, and inspiration.

"It's a curious word, *producing*, because, really, it's all collaboration," he told us. "Many times I've seen producers looking over a musician's shoulder, literally watching his hands. And after a while the musician can't even move his hands anymore because that sort of observation is diminishing. It cuts people off from their potential."

"Trust is the essential element," he said. "If the artist doesn't trust the producer, it diminishes and disempowers the producer, and he's not able to help the artist anymore. If the producer doesn't trust the artist, it debilitates the artist. So without trust, there's no point in even entering into a collaboration."

When he first made records, T Bone wrote out every part for every instrument because he could hear it all in his head—and so thought he knew exactly what he wanted. But he had a moment much like Michael's experience at IDEO, where he realized that he was limiting his partners. Working with the great gospel drummer Billy Maxwell, he was overdirecting, and Billy stopped and said: "If you know exactly what you want, why don't you just play it yourself?" The words weren't antagonistic or even frustrated; they were forthright and factual.

"Here I was telling him what to do, and Billy was about ten thousand times the musician that I was. That was fifty years ago, and I've never forgotten it. It changed how I think. I came to realize that producing a record is, in a sense, like taking a photograph. You want to see the person's best angle. You want to get the light the best for them, or you want to catch them in a moment of absolute honesty."

There are many ways to find an artist's best angle, but T Bone insists that it has less to do with the practice than with the individual.

"It doesn't have to do with the note somebody plays, or even whether they sing in tune or not. I've said for years that I don't care what anybody plays, I just care who's playing it. I want that person to put all of his love and his whole self, his whole heart, into what he's doing. And then the idea from that is that you listen as hard as you can to draw out the best performance from an artist, instead of looking over his shoulder to make sure he's doing it right."

Coming from T Bone, this is no small epiphany. His career is marked by an incredible ability to find and capture authentic moments from artists. One shining example is the 2007 album *Raising Sand*, which united Led Zeppelin front man Robert Plant and bluegrass ingenue Alison Krauss. In a review of the record, NPR said that, although they were an unlikely pair, "they share a keening, a longing in their voices that strips these rock and country songs right back to their haunted souls."

T Bone's hand is apparent but never heavy throughout the album, guiding the artists to find a tone of authenticity without ever seeming to try too hard. Plant and Krauss admit that they struggled to give the songs a fair translation of their delicacy and emotive elements; Krauss said that she felt squeamish and "too white" to sing "Let Your Loss Be Your Lesson," one of the most bluesy songs; T Bone simply encouraged her to sing the song with as much soul as she puts into her bluegrass albums. Both artists continually opened themselves up to T Bone's direction, pushing them outside familiar comfort zones. Plant has openly said that the album changed his career, from a swaggering rock star to one who honors the American music that shaped him.

As producer and creative director, T Bone felt that his role was to build trust, inspire Plant and Krauss, and help them connect to their first loves.

"Listening to Led Zeppelin, what I heard was not only hard rock, I heard Eddie Cochran, Buddy Holly, Skip James, and Robert Johnson. And I knew Alison liked AC/DC. In her voice, I could hear a whole other approach to bluegrass that had never existed because she grew up at a different time in a place where everybody was listening to Molly Hatchet, all those kind of songs. So I approached those two people as creating a synthesis from a place of pure tone—what was his tone of voice and what was her tone of voice—and where did that Venn diagram happen between them? Where did that blend happen between those two mystical tones? Underneath the genre, or whatever you call those things, whatever word you want to use to call those categories, is pure tone, right?"

Echoing words that Hank had said, above, T Bone continued: "First, you have to be able to identify their authentic selves. This takes experience, that takes reading. When I first worked with Gillian Welch, I gave her Sophocles to read. Because it's all there, the roots of drama. The more well read you are, the more you've paid attention to the creative process, the more insight you have. It takes looking at paintings, having a broad view of what creativity is, and it takes a lot of listening. If you're dealing with a music artist, it takes a tremendous amount of listening to a wide range of different kinds of music from different places and different approaches."

At this point in our interview, he dove into his laptop, wanting to play us a song he had been listening to recently. Posted online by a digital archivist group called Dust and Digital, the song was a blues field recording from 1968, captured by Bill Ferris. "I Wish I Was a Jaybird in the Air" is a spoken-word blues tale by Scott Dunbar that tells the story of a man who visits the home of his would-be paramour, equipped with a bottle of moonshine and a chicken. He distracts the mother with the moonshine and the father with the chicken so that he can sneak off with his girl. The song is long and laconic, more than five minutes, and as we sat with T Bone, his delight in it was apparent. The simple, beautiful melody; the stripped-back instrumentation; the call and repeat of the chorus; the raucous laughter from his audience that forces Dunbar to stop, at one point, to laugh along. Halfway through the recording, we realized that T Bone was effortlessly, without any coercion, inviting us into his process. He was looking for the moment and inviting us to explore with him. And the longer we sat together, the more we appreciated the moment. It was a remarkable example of leadership as invitation, of bringing others into a shared experience, shining a spotlight on something that is inspirational, enjoying and exploring it together without an agenda. "That piece has 1,300 views on YouTube," he said. "It's not Katy Perry or Drake, but in my view, it has much more value as an artifact for our culture and our society and our country than anything on the Top 40. Maybe there's something there: the more times something is seen, the less it exists. There's an upside-downiness about so much of modern culture. We love the value of the moment, of the important moment."

This wisdom underpins so much of what we're discussing in this book. In an era where, as Chance the Rapper said, "technology moves faster than business and music moves faster than technology," we believe that musicians who know how to stay ahead of the beat can demystify the process as they're forced to find new ways to adapt to accelerating change. But there's also something about enjoying, capturing, savoring, and preserving the moments that matter too.

"Technology creates efficiencies. That's all it does. Aldous Huxley said that technology is just a faster way of doing ignorant things. Art is the opposite of efficient; efficiency has nothing to do with art. Inspiration is not efficient. It's like the wind: we can't see the wind, but we see it blow the trees, and sometimes it blows the trees down, sometimes it blows a tree onto your house. That's the biggest part of the job: reconnecting an artist to her first love, to get her inspired."

This might sound, as southerners might say, highfalutin'. But for T Bone, it's a two-way street.

"People are always sending me ideas, projects. But the reality is that if we are open, we all do that for each other. Elvis Costello has produced me as a producer for thirty years. He's been my producer. When we were making his album *Spike*, I had gotten very systematized. I would tend to create a loop; a loop gives you a tremendous amount of freedom because every performance can be intercut with every other performance in any place because there are no variances in tempo. In one sense, it creates freedom, but it also eliminates freedom by setting boundaries. Elvis liked that because I don't think he had worked with loops before. But he would also try to subvert the loop in some way."

This goes deeper than the common business trope of "managing up" as well as "managing down." It's a picture of mutual respect with each collaborator bringing a contribution to the table, as well as an openness to having the other person break apart that contribution and rebuild it together. In fact, for T Bone, the process or system isn't the point; it's more about the people. Over and over again, he reiterated that a glorification of systems over personal experience, personal expression, personal connection sells us all short. Genres, preordained systems, and well-documented methodologies can bring a benefit, but not if they undermine the opportunity to create and capture a meaningful moment.

"When I worked with Gregg Allman on *Low Country Blues*, I listened to all of Gregg's past work. I knew his work anyway, but I went through the exercise of imagining the first records he liked, the first song he heard on the radio, the first song he wrote, what his parents listened to in the house when he was growing up. And then I put together what I thought might be a history for him, thirty or forty songs to choose material from. And he wrote back to me: 'You're not supposed to know me so well.'"

T Bone went through the same exercise with Jeff Bridges to develop the character of Bad Blake in *Crazy Heart*. He told us that the idea is to go back to an artist's core and build around that, rather than to draw on some trip they took to Morocco in 1978 or Hollywood in 1982.

"Those are perfectly important and fine, but they aren't the truest part of who the artist is. I'm looking for their first love, and it overlaps with what I love, what we're both doing with our whole hearts. That's the wellspring of music."

For fifty years, T Bone has been searching for these moments of resonance, artist by artist. Honesty, he says, is a key to authenticity.

"One thing I can say for certain is you can never, ever lie or hype someone you're collaborating with because we're all incredibly sensitive, especially in a collaborative or artistic endeavor. People will know the moment you're hyping them. Even if they don't consciously register it, they'll feel it on a cellular level."

When Panos was leading an executive education program with ESADE business school on Berklee's campus in Valencia, Spain, he saw this kind of empathetic leadership in action. He asked Pablo Munguía—a program director at the college who has helmed engineering for Super Bowl halftime shows, the Grammy

Awards, and the Oscars—to join him. The goal was to demonstrate how producers approach talent, coaxing out the best performance. There was a sound booth in the room, with a young singer inside, seated in front of a microphone. Watching Pablo work was mind-blowing, how he created trust between himself and the singer but also in the artist himself, building confidence through encouragement without false praise. They did take after take, and in each instance, Pablo acted as chief empath, focusing on what the singer did well and how to build upon it rather than the mistakes made.

Afterward, Panos led a conversation with the executives about what they could learn when it comes to managing people, and the word that the attendees used most often to describe what they had seen was "trust." Trust in your own abilities, trust between the producer and talent, shaping the environment rather than trying to shape the person—and the improvement in performance that everyone could hear. Think for a moment about managers you have had, or perhaps even the manager you have been. Do you start with an assumption of trust, or an absence of trust that employees have to earn? If someone is struggling to get up to speed, is that their problem? And what sort of magic can happen when you get to witness someone who is tentative become confident?

"This applies not only to music, to art. In anything, there has to be trust to remove fear," T Bone said. "In business, employees fear that if they step over a line, they're going to lose their paycheck, they're going to have to figure out another way to feed their children. And I almost hate to use this word, but it's fascism. You can't lessen people in order to control them. It's possible to trust, not the process, but people. I don't care what notes people play as much as the person who's playing them."

Finding (and Shaping) the Way Forward

Once you have mastered a mindset of helping others to succeed, it's surprisingly applicable at scale. And who better to ask about this than Jimmy Iovine, the Interscope megaproducer we introduced in Chapter 1? From his work with musicians in recording studios to his cofounding of Beats by Dre, to his role creating Apple Music, his leadership of artists and collaborators has been underpinned by a consistent philosophy of self-awareness, understanding the individual, and management of the environment rather than the person.

A few weeks after we talked with Hank, we sat down with Jimmy.

"I come from Brooklyn. We were a working-class family, a nice family," he told us. "My father was a longshoreman. When I started working in music production, I showed up with a lot of goodwill, a lot of energy, but without a lot of information."

One day, while walking past his father's social club, Jimmy overheard his father talking to a friend outside. "The guy asks my dad, 'What is it with your son, with the music and the headphones? What is this shit he does?' My dad goes, 'He's got magic ears. He can hear what you're thinking.'"

But Jimmy, who was only twenty-one years old at the time, was not only a rare talent; he also had an incredible amount of good fortune. In the first five years of his career, he recorded six albums: three with John Lennon, two with Bruce Springsteen, and one with Patti Smith.

"That was my college education, and it was extraordinary," he told us. "I hadn't developed a philosophy yet. My brain was open, and I relearned everything I knew as a kid, taking everything I learned from those three artists and records. With artists like that in the room, I would just listen, get to know them, get in their heads, and find out what they wanted to do. My job was to help them do it. Today, record producers are the guys who write all the music. That's not what I was doing."

By his midtwenties, he had developed a skill set that gave him incredible fluidity in his own career: listening, coming to a deep understanding of his collaborators, shifting between roles of leading and following, possessing a relentless willingness to experiment, and knowing how all of these work best when working with the right partners. For Jimmy, this list included Tom Petty, Stevie Nicks, Dire Straits, and U2. When asked about collaborating with David Geffen—the legendary founder of Asylum Records, Geffen Records, DGC Records, and the film studio DreamWorks—Jimmy once said: "I play mental games with myself. David and I disagree a lot. I bet on his answer a little more than my own. I say: 'This guy's really smart. I think he's completely wrong, but I'm going to try it anyway.'"

This is a lesson for all of us, in any career. Work with talented people who have a vision of their own, get to know them well, and learn how to get the best out of them.

"Steve [Jobs] surrounded himself with the right people, but as the head of the company, he also knew what their limits were," he told us. "He knew what their talents were but also what they weren't good at. Just because someone is called the head of marketing doesn't mean that they do every part of marketing right. That's what the entrepreneur has to know. I don't care where you go, Apple, Google, Facebook. If you have an idea and you give it to a collaborator, you need to have a feel, appreciation, for what the other person brings."

John Lennon, Bruce Springsteen, Patti Smith, Tom Petty, Stevie Nicks, U2. Jimmy is acutely aware that his experience is as remarkable as it is rare, but he also believes that the lessons he learned about producing and leadership can be applied at scale. So after Apple acquired Beats for $3 billion, he and Dr. Dre cofounded an academy at the University of Southern California—to give students the sort of opportunity they never had in their youth. The USC Jimmy Iovine and Andre Young Academy was conceived as an educational start-up, designed to disrupt by positioning academic learning at the intersection of four essential areas: art and design, engineering and computer science, business and venture management, and communications.

"Founding the academy, I was entering yet another phase of my life with very little information," Jimmy told us. "I didn't go to college and neither did Dre. So what did we know? We knew that we hated school and felt comfortable assuming that a lot of kids hate school. And what we've seen is a lot of high school kids saying: 'Why would I go to college? What will it do for me?' It's a valid question. The world changed; college didn't."

At the academy, students work in cross-disciplinary teams throughout their entire college experience. Professors from different concentrations communicate with one another and coteach classes. From day one, the academy's students understand the particular value and contribution of other disciplines, what they bring to the table. It's a bit like the way a good musician understands collaborators who play different instruments. A guitarist might never have played with a particular drummer before, but he understands how drummers think, knows how they can watch for and find each other in a song. Just as importantly, by the time they graduate, students from the academy have developed a language for communicating with other disciplines.

"That's why Dre and I put up $70 million for the academy," Jimmy told us. "We could have started a program at USC for free, give students a little of this, a little of that. Use what is already there and add an art class. But that's not the idea. I look at new jobs and think: Why don't people understand what other disciplines are about and how to communicate with them? That's not what is happening in most colleges, but in our school it is."

"In my companies, I wanted designers who could communicate with engineers," he continued. "You don't have to be an engineer, but if you've studied alongside engineers, worked on projects together while learning your own job, you understand their 'why' as well as their language. I think we're building more expanded people, who have a lot more flexibility in what they do, giving them a real advantage."

Teaming up with Laurene Powell Jobs, Steve's widow, Jimmy has helped take this idea one step further: into high schools with XQ Institute. With the guidance of board members, including Iovine, Geoffrey Canada, Marc Eckō, Michael Klein, and Yo-Yo Ma, XQ Institute has established six design principles: strong mission and culture; meaningful, engaged learning; caring, trusting relationships; youth voice and choice; smart use of time, space, and tech; and community partnerships. The organization works in communities across America, with individual public schools and public-school systems, to encourage big dreams about what high school can be. And just as importantly, to turn ideas into innovation, creating school experiences that are both more rigorous and more equitable.

In Jimmy's own career, he had four different jobs: record producer, cofounder of a record company, cofounder of a headphone company, and head of a streaming service. In some ways, his story parallels the history of an industry battling with technology—the record labels at first resisting digital formats and then trying to battle the internet, bringing lawsuits left and right, before finally embracing streaming services. When, in 2019, the *New York Times* asked Jimmy if the music business had recovered from the disruption of Napster, if the problem had been solved, he replied:

> I don't view it as a problem solved. There's been progress, but there's a way to go yet. If I were still at Interscope, here are the things I'd be worried about. I'd be worried that I don't have a direct relationship with my consumer. The artists and the streaming platforms do.
>
> I didn't want [technology] to be the "other side." I wanted it to be all one thing. I wasn't bailing on music. I always thought that technology was going to get people to listen to music in a better way, and you were going to promote it all through a streaming service. But it would all be in the same house.

He admitted that he had not figured out how to continue to push the industry forward. He told the *Times*: "There are some clues. Have we entered into an age of music where artists are afraid to alienate people? Since the country is so polarized, am I afraid to alienate the other audience? Am I afraid to alienate a sponsor from my Instagram? I don't know. I'm asking the question."

But one thing that was clear when we spoke: even in his retirement from business, with his work in schools, Jimmy is still listening to what his partners and consumers have to say and creating space for them to share their vision. And he is confident that young people will lead the way forward, especially if they are as prepared as the academy's graduates.

"The kids coming out of the academy are great; they get tons of job offers. I took [Snap Inc. CEO] Evan Spiegel there, and he said to me: 'Jimmy, if this was a school when I was in college I would have stayed in college,' he told us. 'If I were at AT&T and Warner, right now, I would hire all twenty-five students of the academy's next graduating class.' Big corporations need employees who are knowledgeable in multiple disciplines. If we can prove the model then we can scale it, put it in all schools, especially in places where kids need better opportunities. Creating not just opportunities, but an advantage."

The Next Evolution Has Already Started

Let's look at this question from the flip side: the corporate landscape of brands, products, and marketing. Advertising and music industry entrepreneur Steve Stoute most recently caught the world's attention with a $70 million investment from Alphabet Inc., Andreessen Horowitz, and 21st Century Fox to launch UnitedMasters, a new music venture. His résumé includes working as an executive at Sony Music and Interscope Geffen A&M; founding creative agency Translation, which connects the world's most famous brands to culture through sports and entertainment;

and authoring the book *The Tanning of America: How Hip-Hop Created a Culture that Rewrote the Rules of the New Economy*. According to Jay-Z, Steve is "the conduit between corporate America and rap and the streets—he speaks both languages."

We spoke with him as spring turned toward summer in 2020 about shaping a multidisciplinary workforce and how art and commerce overlap—whether in the recording studio, the marketing agency, the boardroom, or everyday business interactions, Stoute isn't just a seasoned entrepreneur. Before launching his marketing businesses, he was an executive at both Sony and Interscope Geffen A&M, a manager for Nas and Mary J. Blige, and a producer of soundtracks for *Wild Wild West* and *8 Mile*. He gets the best out of people by helping them play to their strengths, not their job titles.

"I think that we are far too often victims of the box we were put in. In order for you to know what somebody 'does,' you put them in a uniform, which is their job. There was a period of time when this was great because you could excel at your job, be accepted as your job, expect payment uniformity, security, blah, blah, blah. But things have changed. With so much free-form thinking and the ability for everyone to access so much, we're seeing that dissipate. The ideas of who an artist is and what an entrepreneur is are evolving."

At Translation, where he still serves as CEO, jobs are both defined and fluid because every employee is asked to declare a major, which is their primary role at the agency, as well as a minor, which is their strongest passion. What, Steve asks, would they be doing if money didn't matter? Not only does this encourage cross-disciplinary connections, but it also creates new opportunities for clients. When a creative brief makes its way through the company, employees look for peripheral dimensions based on their passions, and if they can contribute to the project they are pulled onto its team.

The result is a new kind of team, with a new version of intelligence. It's not about rewriting rules, because in a very real sense there aren't any rules. With UnitedMasters, Steve is creating a data- and technology-driven services company that provides tools for creators to maximize their potential while remaining independent of the traditional record label model. Not only are they disrupting an industry, they are creating a new one.

"In an agency, the culture people are always the ones who are way too cool, who don't want to dumb down the currency of a brand. The tech people are the nerds and only collaborate with other tech people. And the storytellers are very protective of their work. But when all three come together, you see magic come out of it. So we consider culture, technology, and storytelling to be a single organism. We hire engineers who are fascinated by the music business, who are dialed into what is going on in culture. We hire storytellers who see technology as a way to amplify their stories. Everybody needs to be prolific at two or three of these things. That's the company of tomorrow."

Steve has applied this same thinking to his work pairing brands with celebrities, encouraging artists to identify and articulate their own vision and values authentically to connect with consumers.

"In the '80s, artists said: 'I'm not doing this shit at all. I'm not touching product, that's not cool.' It was like working with the Man, the corporation. Then hip-hop became the first art form to say: 'You know what? It's all about making money, and I'll do what makes sense to make money.'"

But far too often, artist-brand partnerships were what Steve calls "putting ketchup on a bad idea." A brand spends money for a celebrity to hold a product in proximity to their face. But the relationship is hollow, and consumers can tell.

"That formula was flawed for all of the obvious reasons," he told us. "Musicians rejected it because they felt that if they engaged in corporate marketing tactics, they'd lose credibility as an artist. It failed brands because the partnerships failed to show shared values. Nobody believed that there was anything in common between the brand and the artist or athlete."

So some brands went further, offering creative director titles to an artist.

"They give titles as a way to induce them into partnership because it appeals to the ego," Steve said. "I think of Tiger Woods and Buick. Clearly it doesn't work at all; it was a legacy relationship. Or Lady Gaga and Polaroid. You see so many of these partnerships not having value. They don't have much to talk about, and they fade."

But Steve knew, as a music and advertising executive, that when an artist peels back the curtain, authentically showing his values and working only with brands that are aligned, it can be powerful. It takes a special set of skills to bring out the best in an artist, but those skills are applicable to every industry in the current business environment. Not only applicable but invaluable. Our ability to adapt to, and work with, many different disciplines and personalities expands not only their potential but our own, as well as that of our companies. And our willingness to listen with our eyes closed, to manage environments so others can explore their authentic vision and passion—in other words, to both lead and follow—will help us connect with customers.

Throughout this chapter, and indeed throughout the chapters before and following, we have seen the importance of being a polymath in today's business world. Pharrell shapes songs and designs sneakers; Imogen Heap's self-expression takes form not only in the studio but in blockchain start-ups; Hank talked about CEOs who are also DJs. As business leaders who manage employees and teachers working at the collegiate level, we are acutely aware of a gap in the educational system—the same realization that led Jimmy Iovine and Dr. Dre to found their academy. Schooling that makes kids into math geniuses but is absent of humanity leads to employees who can create algorithms without regard for their societal impact. We fully support advances in STEAM, in artificial intelligence, and in big data, but developing creative capacity is sadly absent in today's conversation around education. We need citizens and leaders who are driven by curiosity, by the desire to learn, experiment, collaborate, and explore. Curiosity is core; it's critical. If you are curious, you learn; if you learn, you push yourself to be exposed to new ideas and practices. If you do that then you live outside your comfort zone, and living outside your comfort zone grows empathy.

Saying that "art is the answer" could sound trite, even insulting. We're not claiming to have the answer; in fact, we believe that building the creative capacity is key to solving very real, practical, and even life-threatening problems that plague our society. Take a step back and consider: What if our leaders, whether in business or in elected offices, viewed their chief role as removing obstacles, building trust, and creating the right conditions for other people to thrive? And what would the world look like if we taught our young people to value and explore curiosity, to look for inspiration in others, to get outside their comfort zones and grow in empathy?

Efficient systems are important. But if they are the lone hallmark of our society, of how we interact with collaborators and co-workers at the expense of continued curiosity, then something real is lost. After all, creativity and imagination are what separate us from other species.

When we raised this topic with T Bone, he paused before responding. "In the past century, decisions were made around systems. For example, the school system, decisions were made about the most efficient way to teach children that stripped art out of education. But systems can outlive their usefulness by decades or centuries and keep running well past their expiration date, when they should have been discarded. As a society, I think we've glorified systems to the point that when those systems are challenged, it's almost like we have no idea what to do."

But this is where creativity comes in. As producers, managers, and leaders, we can create space and remove obstacles so talented people can explore ideas and draw on inspiration, and we can all move forward together.

"In any management position or administrative position, by distrusting the people you're trying to help, you create insecurity," he told us. "If the artist doesn't trust the producer, it diminishes and disempowers the producer, and he's not able to help the artist anymore." Then, as if he were summing up our entire chapter in one sentence, he added: "To distrust people you're working with disempowers them, but to trust them empowers them."

Interlude 5

T Bone told us that all American pop music can be traced back to the Fisk Jubilee Singers, an a cappella African American ensemble of Fisk University students formed in 1871. Within two years, they became global pop stars, performing spirituals, blues, and parlor songs for both Ulysses S. Grant in Washington, DC, and Queen Victoria in London. This playlist features songs produced by Hank Shocklee, Jimmy Iovine, and T Bone Burnett that build on this heritage by blending the genres both lyrically and musically.

Hank Shocklee
POISON, Bell Biv DeVoe
JUICE, Eric B. & Rakim
TOMORROW PEOPLE, Ziggy Marley and the Wailers
Jimmy Iovine
ANGEL OF HARLEM, U2
DON'T GET ME WRONG, Pretenders
BECAUSE THE NIGHT, Patti Smith
T Bone Burnett
SUBZERO FUN, Autolux
RICH WOMAN, Robert Plant and Alison Krauss
ONE DAY LATE, Sam Phillips
LOST, Cassandra Wilson

Deep Listening: Listen to the soundtrack from the 2009 film *Crazy Heart*, a musical personae Burnett and Jeff Bridges developed from the imagined influences of the main character Bad Blake. Can you name them?

six
connecting

Share Your Imagination

What you must understand is that my voice comes from the
energy of the audience. The better they are, the better I get.

—Freddie Mercury

On July 13, 1985, Freddie Mercury gave the performance of his
lifetime. If you watched the movie *Bohemian Rhapsody*, with its
twenty-one-minute recreation of the legendary set at Live Aid, one
of the biggest rock concerts in history, you saw something close to
the original. But the Hollywood version wasn't quite as magical—
in part because there was a subtext that was overlooked on screen.
When Queen took the stage, they weren't the main attraction. In
fact, their popularity had fizzled, and the concert boasted some of
the biggest names of the day, including Led Zeppelin, the Who,

and Elton John; Queen was sandwiched between up-and-comers U2 and the legendary David Bowie. But Mercury delivered a show that is widely considered to be the greatest rock performance of all-time. With supernatural energy and confidence, he belted out seven of the band's greatest hits, strutting across the stage like it had been constructed just for him.

In a memorial review of the concert, written thirty-three years later by Holly Thomas, a CNN journalist who was not even born when Live Aid took place, Freddie is the highlight.

> Past their peak and reeling from the catastrophe of a misadvised run of shows in apartheid South Africa the previous year, Queen was not expected to shine. Mercury, in particular, had been the focus of disparaging coverage and rumors in the press, where speculation over his sexuality had arguably choked the band's attempts to break into the American market. Amid an atmosphere charged with pessimism, Mercury danced out on stage and welcomed the crowd like his dearest friend. By the time he sat down at the piano and hit the first few notes of "Bohemian Rhapsody," he was the absolute master of the stadium. Over the next 21 minutes, his audience, and the 1.9 billion people watching on TV around the world, fell in love with him. His humor, his hyper-masculine yet fantastically camp energy and that phenomenal four octave voice were irresistible.

The only moment of quiet came when Mercury stood at the edge of the stage, leading the crowd in a long vocal improvisation that came to be known as "the note heard around the world." He sang to the crowd a long "ayyyy-oooo," and seventy-two thousand people echoed it back to him. He repeated the phrase, showcasing his incredible vocal range, then held his sawed-off mic stand toward the audience, and they sang it back (as best they could!) over and over again with a single voice.

Twenty-two years later, Steve Jobs made the most memorable appearance of his career when he unveiled the first iPhone at MacWorld. His presentation had all of the qualities of an unforgettable concert: playing the crowd favorites, using rhetorical flourishes, and then launching into his latest release with bold passion.

He started by telling the four thousand people in attendance: "Every once in a while, a revolutionary product comes along that changes everything . . . we're going to make some history together today." He played his greatest hits, reminding the crowd that nearly a quarter century earlier, he had introduced the revolutionary Macintosh computer and later the first iPod, which changed not only how people listen to music but the entire music industry.

In the lead-up to unveiling his newest innovation, he repeated a variation of the line "Today, Apple is going to reinvent the phone" five times, amplifying anticipation. Everyone was on the edge of their seats when he said: "Today we're introducing three revolutionary products of this class. The first one is a widescreen iPod with touch controls. The second is a revolutionary mobile phone. And the third is a breakthrough internet communications device. . . . An iPod, a phone, and an internet communicator. An iPod, a phone, are you getting it? These are not three separate devices, this is one device, and we are calling it iPhone. Today, Apple is going to reinvent the phone, and here it is."

Up on the screen flashed a clunky, outdated, bastardized beast of technology, opposite in every way of the iPhone's minimal design. The crowd laughed, and Jobs had them in the palm of his hand as he walked through the features and differences of his product before finally giving the world the first viewing of the phone that transformed how people talk, listen, look, and interact.

His presentation was compelling because he was sharing his enthusiasm, as well as his product, with the audience. Jobs believed in his vision for technology and created a magical space focused on a seemingly magical product. This wasn't just a product launch; it was a moment of revelation. The future was being born in that very moment.

Get Their Attention, Then Bring the Goods

In this age of digital music, more than twenty-four thousand songs are uploaded to the Web every day. The artists behind each track want one thing, fans, and often resort to outlandish and shocking performances to gain likes and shares. Madonna inspired generations of singers to leave their clothes backstage, Kanye West stole Taylor Swift's microphone, and Cardi B savaged the president. Sometimes these performances are an organic part of their artistic process; at others, they are strategic moves made in collaboration with managers and marketing teams. Either way, musicians understand that there's nothing like a spectacle to generate buzz.

Legendary manager Shep Gordon is a maestro at creating spectacles. He cut his teeth in the late 1960s and over the course of his career managed Pink Floyd, Blondie, Rick James, Kenny Loggins, even Groucho Marx. His first worldwide success came when promoting Alice Cooper, one of America's first shock rockers. Cooper wanted to reshape his image from the hippie who hung out with Jimi Hendrix and Janis Joplin and turned to Gordon for help. Their goal? To make every parent in the country forbid their children from going to an Alice Cooper concert. They used cartoonish Satanic imagery for album covers, created a giant penis out of a fire extinguisher for Cooper to shoot off during live performances, and even faked an explosion during a press conference, with Cooper being rushed to the hospital in a rented ambulance by friends dressed as EMTs.

Next, they turned their sights overseas. Gordon booked a ten-thousand-seat venue in London, but with the concert days away, they had sold only fifty tickets. As Gordon sat watching British television one morning, he realized that the best megaphone for his message was the morning news, specifically the helicopters that covered rush hour traffic. In his press materials, he had a photograph of Cooper naked, wearing only a snake, so he enlarged the image and pasted it to the side of a tractor-trailer truck. Then he ordered its driver to navigate through traffic to Piccadilly Circus, one of the busiest roundabouts in London, and break down. He had planted an enormous billboard of his rock star, naked, to be broadcast to every breakfast table in the country. The stunt had its desired effect: Alice Cooper was on the lips of every parent, who was as outraged as Gordon had hoped.

"There are artists that come through in every generation who see it," Gordon told *The Knowledge Project* podcast in 2019. "You look at Lady Gaga today. She's exactly what Alice was forty years ago. I think it's basically the same. Just the economics changed, the delivery system changed, but it's the same kind of thing. It's just figuring out how to get attention and then having the real goods behind the curtain."

Years later, Gordon applied his talent for promotion to a new industry. He had sobered up, replacing his heavy drug use with a love for cooking and food. A new idea dawned on him: Why weren't chefs celebrities?

"I got to see how poorly the chefs of the world were treated," he said. "French chefs were treated better than anywhere else in the world [but] the treatment that American chefs got compared to him was different than in France [and] they were great artists . . . I thought: I've spent my whole life monetizing artists. I sort of know how to do this. I'm going to change the direction of these careers."

Gordon began taking on chef clients. Among them was Emeril Lagasse, for whom Gordon negotiated a daytime show on the Food Network. Emeril came into *Emeril Live!* with a down-to-earth, fun-loving personality. His famous catchphrases like "Bam!" "Kick it up a notch!" and "It ain't rocket science!"—old favorites in his restaurant kitchens—translated perfectly to television audiences. Soon he had a huge fan base: at the show's peak, it was watched in more than 250,000 households every day.

You might not be ready for a talk show or to cause traffic jams with gigantic naked photos, but there's something instructive here. In the corporate world, we often think that we need to persuade others with intellectual rigor rather than a visceral response. But intuition and confidence can be just as powerful, when it comes to connecting with an audience, as facts and figures.

We've lived this, seen it happen. In 2001, after a few years of entrepreneurial exploration, Michael cofounded a company called Tricycle with three friends. Their objective was to replace samples in the commercial carpet industry with digital simulations printed on paper. Carpet sampling might not sound as sexy as a sold-out concert, but Tricycle's technology became a game changer, saving manufacturers millions of dollars while exponentially reducing oil use and landfill waste.

Yet, despite the accuracy of the images, none of the carpet industry executives would return their calls because nobody *believed* that simulated samples on paper would look realistic enough to replace actual pieces of carpet made from nylon yarn. So they hatched a plan: use angel funding to drive to Chicago to the world's largest annual trade fair for interiors products and put on a show.

The setup was a lot like getting ready for a gig, stage and lights included. For the exhibit, Michael designed a three-by-three-foot wooden platform that held four actual pieces of carpet. Over them, they built cantilevered aluminum canopies designed to control lighting, a critical component for perceiving color. Then the team carefully placed a single paper simulation on top of the carpet, aligning it perfectly with the pattern. When you stepped back, you couldn't tell where the nylon ended and the paper began.

With the stage ready, they needed a performance that would guide audiences into disbelief and build anticipation. When a carpet executive walked past Tricycle's booth, Michael started the performance:

> Tricycle: Do you use carpet samples in your day-to-day business?
>
> Mr. Carpet: Yeah, we use them to perfect a product's design before we launch it to market.
>
> Tricycle: How many rounds of samples do you go through?
>
> Mr. Carpet: Oh, dozens. Sometimes way more.
>
> Tricycle: And what do you do with the samples when you're finished?
>
> Mr. Carpet: Well, they go to the landfill.
>
> Tricycle: What if a paper sample could replace them, at least in the early rounds of product design?
>
> Mr. Carpet: It's a nice idea, but the color and pattern would never look right. I need to see the real thing to know if it's going to work.
>
> Tricycle: What if I told you that you've already seen them?

As they leaned close to the display, they shook their heads, still skeptical. They would pick up one corner of the paper sample or run their fingers across it to make sure it wasn't an illusion. Michael had built up their disbelief through the dialogue, setting up an aha moment. Nothing was different about the product: it was already good enough. But without the reveal, the impact would have been minimal. Michael and the team left the trade show with a business card from every major commercial carpet manufacturer and the realization that no stage is too small for a great performance.

Making It Personal

Ask any entrepreneur for his list of top-ten business idols, and chances are good that Richard Branson will make the cut. The original bad boy of business and founder of the Virgin Group, Branson knows how to work a crowd. He famously wore a female flight attendant's uniform, complete with lipstick, to help promote

Virgin Airlines and then repeated the stunt in a wedding dress for the launch of Virgin Brides. To promote Virgin Cola, he drove a Sherman tank through Times Square, crushing a wall of Coca-Cola cans. Here he's rappelling down a skyscraper; there he's a human bowling ball. The buzz that he created around the Virgin brands helped drive revenue, but Branson's real power comes from his personality, his emotional makeup. His unguarded enthusiasm shines as much as the sincerity of his effort to make life better for his customers.

When he stepped into a new frontier with Spaceport America, a launching pad for private space shuttles, it seemed like a natural progression. Part of his appeal is his willingness to take personal risks, not only by hanging from a helicopter but by making enormous pivots in his business, from music retail into hotels, mobile phones, festivals, and films. His bold and flamboyant moves inspire people. It's no exaggeration to say that Branson should be credited for shifting how people think about what a business can be and what a businessperson is supposed to do. We know that he is driven by something bigger than profit and are rooting for him to take on his next and more ambitious project. Private space travel? If anyone can pull it off, it's Richard Branson.

Building your organization around your personality may have pitfalls, but it can also provide you with new opportunities and accountability. Branson has used his personal appeal to champion humanitarian causes around the world. In recent years, he has played a role in persuading the president of Uganda to veto a bill written to outlaw homosexuality in the country. He has stated that money isn't that useful except as a way to transform the world. "A business is simply an idea to make other people's lives better," he has said. "If you aren't making a positive difference to other people's lives, you shouldn't be in business."

Kiran Gandhi, who goes by Madame Gandhi, is another entrepreneur who connects with audiences at a deeply personal level through her business ventures, her activism, and her music. For her, *the personal is political is professional*; there is no separation. Raised in New York and Bombay, Gandhi—whose first name means "first light of the sun in the morning" in Hindi and Sanskrit—triple-majored in mathematics, political science, and women's studies at Georgetown University. Then she earned an MBA at Harvard Business School, while also touring as a drummer with Academy Award–nominated British Tamil rapper M.I.A.

When we first met Madame Gandhi, she wasn't on the large festival stages she now plays. She was at a start-up Demo Day in Boston. She had just spent eight weeks in an experimental design venture that combined expertise from IDEO, Fidelity Bank, and Harvard's i-Lab (Innovation Lab) to explore new concepts for blockchain and was presenting a business concept. As we watched her click through her slides, she was compelling and engaging, speaking in a rhythmic cadence, with confidence and enthusiasm.

The following year we heard more about her, along with the rest of the world, when she ran the London Marathon while on her period, without a pad or tampon, to the astonishment of all. Photographs of her crossing the finish line with bloody leggings filled news and social media feeds. In the many interviews that followed, Gandhi said that she made the choice to run for herself first and then decided to use the moment to call attention to period shaming and other stigmas that women face globally.

"For the run, I made a decision about my own comfort that would best enable me to complete the 26.2 miles," she wrote in an article for the UK's *Independent* newspaper. "And yet, because we don't talk about this very natural monthly process, my decision shocked many people."

In the article, she goes on to describe how the lives of women are impacted by secrecy around their periods and how this attitude toward menstruation is indicative of a much bigger issue. "Women are taught to be quiet about our emotions, hide them away, be very secretive about when we're happy or sad," she said. "Being female and being strong doesn't mean you don't talk about your emotions, and it also doesn't mean that you act stronger than you are."

Branson's motivation is commercial, underpinned by the personal. Madame Gandhi's starts personally and then extends to the commercial. A desire to amplify justice and equity drives everything she does: after receiving so much attention around an issue that she finds personally important, she began to feel that she should seize the moment to spread her message of female empowerment through a medium of her choosing. And she chose her life-long love: music. She had been playing piano from an early age, but it was a New York City school bus driver who changed her perspective on what music can mean. When he would pull up to a bus stop and open the folding doors, parents heard the sounds of classical music. But as soon as the kids were on board and the door closed, he switched to the local hip-hop station. According to Gandhi, who was in kindergarten at the time, he wanted the students to experience a different side to their education, which they might not get otherwise. "Listening to Nas and Lauryn Hill," she told *Billboard* magazine, "it instilled in me a sense of empathy and storytelling I didn't have access to anywhere else."

By the age of eight she had picked up the drumsticks. "Women on the sticks were rare," says the *Billboard* profile, "and she loved the rebelliousness, the freedom of the instrument, a far cry from the right-and-wrong she had previously known on the piano."

Performing as Madame Gandhi, she has released two albums: *Visions* and *Voices*. *Billboard* said of the latter: "A vulnerable wave through the intricacies of love, power, femininity and heartbreak, *Voices* was Gandhi's way of beginning this journey of expression, of showing that what are thought of as traditionally 'female' qualities, so frequently demeaned as weak in both American and global culture, are actually far more powerful than anyone may have dreamed, women themselves included."

"Women are constantly underestimated and pushed around," she said. "We take it because we've grown up being used to that almost, being passed over for opportunities or people not thinking we're as good at reaching our fullest potential as we are. . . . I want to leave the house without someone making fun of my ambition. I want to leave the house feeling safe in my own body. I want to leave the house feeling free and safe enough to voice my own opinion when I have an opinion. It's like, damn, that's the utopia?"

When we asked Gandhi to share her thoughts on feminism, music, and her new line of branded merchandise, it was clear that each of these channels is only a means to an end: connecting with audiences to spread her message.

"It's very validating," she told us, "especially when you're still at a pretty early stage in your career, to have people who say 'I believe in this, I enjoy this, I want to be part of this.' Showing different types of success and different models for success makes me feel like I'm actually making a difference. People love seeing people take a risk and then be successful."

However, she knows that connection is not a one-way street; she has to know her audience, what they want and how to reach them. At the time of our interview, she had recently returned from a tour in India and saw an opportunity to boost revenues from shows that broke even on ticket sales, as well as share important ideas. Many artists consider merchandise an afterthought, but Madame Gandhi decided to work with NorBlack NorWhite, a women-owned clothing brand based in Delhi, to create stunning shirts and jumpsuits out of brightly colored linen, silk, and color-gradient denim.

"Where I was really inspired was by artists who have a major label budget, doing things at a much higher level," she said. "I'm a big fan of Justin Bieber, for example, and he now has an entire clothing line. I was inspired by that and thought: 'I want to sell something for $200 that's built to last and amazing.'"

However, Gandhi knows her audience well enough to understand that this kind of clothing is not for every show, every venue.

"At my album release party, people were happy to buy the expensive stuff because we were showing it in a really elevated way. We photographed it correctly, we had a video, and the pop-up shop was beautiful. It felt like a retail experience. But on the road, it's a totally different thing. People are in a dive bar where it smells like beer. They're not going to spend $300 on a silk dress with a beer in their hand. It's just not part of the flow.

"The journey map of someone going to a show at a club is different. It's already 11:00 p.m.; they already have a couple of drinks in their system. They're down to spend thirty bucks on a shirt because that's what their expectation is."

So she retooled the line to include new products like socks and T-shirts printed with powerful lyrics from her songs: "Let boys be feminine." "The earth is still waiting for us." "Own your voice, don't be afraid."

Through her music and her merch, Madame Gandhi knows how to connect with fans. And, other than onstage, there is nowhere that she shines so brightly as on social media. Instagram and Twitter, when used by brands, can far too often come off as overly contrived, curated, and cold. But when we look at Gandhi's social media presence, we see an amazing record of real life and the radical commitment to authenticity that marks everything she creates.

"It is very important to invest where you can have impact and less where you can nourish your own ego," she said. "When we start out, we want the bigger opportunities, but the truth is that if you are offering something of value, word spreads organically and the bigger opportunities come regardless."

In our conversation, she elaborated on this idea:

"I approach social media from the spiritual or, let's say, inspired mentality," she told us. "On the one hand, there's the argument that you should be posting every day to engage your fans, and there's part of me that does subscribe to that. Of course, you want to stay active and let your social media reflect your activeness in real life. On the other hand, any time I've posted out of necessity, as opposed to out of genuine inspiration and a desire to share something with an audience that I think is worth sharing, it has always failed. It doesn't perform as well. When I genuinely feel inspired, I think the energy is palpable, and that excitedness translates."

During the coronavirus crisis of 2020, we talked with Madame Gandhi again about what it means to connect with people authentically when we are separate. She broke it down, by channel: YouTube and Spotify and IGTV for polished content; SoundCloud and Instagram stories for a more unrefined, raw appeal that fans like to connect with; her blog and website for updates and recaps; Facebook as a large cardboard sign in a coffeehouse.

"I'm excited about exploring platforms," she told us. "The tech community is inspiring; each platform serves a pain point. And they are constantly being improved. It's our responsibility as creators to be brave enough to get onto these sites and take full advantage of them."

The tech, of course, is a means to an end: her passion for building community with her fan base, as well as among LGBTQ+ folks, students, and young women. When we look at her online presence we see a woman who draws together communities of people, always open, always welcoming, out of a desire of advancing a shared agenda. Where so much of cobranding is opportunistic and self-serving, Madame Gandhi has found genuine ways to weave together her passion, art, and livelihood.

"The truth is that I spend so much time alone," she told us. "Time thinking about my speeches, writing down my ideas and practicing them, thinking about how I want to impact each community I am asked to serve, and of course writing music."

This alone-but-not-lonely perspective has deep roots for Gandhi. Since her childhood, she told us, she has not felt that she belongs to any one community, a fact that has enabled her to explore ideas without limits, to think and act independently. This brings enormous value because it enables her to keep her perspective unique and honest, rather than driven by the agendas of others.

"So when I speak at big corporations like Spotify or YouTube or at universities, I can say everything I want to say without feeling I have to curb or curtail my opinion. In this way, my work is valued even more, and I am included and welcomed into that community."

Madame Gandhi is just one example of a new generation of artists who build on their own authentic values and personal drivers to connect with audiences. It's a major shift in a well-established industry and one that Jimmy Iovine saw coming as far back as 2001. He recalled sitting in staff meetings at Interscope, realizing that the entire music business was foundationally flawed.

"The old trick of giving people advances and taking them onto the radio was not enough. It had to change. A lot of these young artists now, they are more native on communication platforms than people working in the labels anyway. They get started on their own, but the labels still think: OK this person has a following; we'll pay $5 million for them."

He pointed to Lil Nas X, an American rapper, singer, and songwriter. Lil Nas X has said that he started out posting short-form comedy videos on Facebook and then moved to Instagram and Twitter. At the same time, he created Nicki Minaj fan accounts featuring flash-fiction style "scenario threads" and using multiple Twitter accounts to artificially make his tweets go viral. His most followed account, @NasMaraj, was suspended by Twitter due to violating spam policies, so he apparently created new accounts, although he later denied having run them. In late October 2018, he purchased a music beat created by Dutch producer YoungKio from an online store for thirty dollars. The beat sampled rock band Nine Inch Nails's track "34 Ghosts IV." Lil Nas X recorded "Old Town Road," the song that would become an international hit in less than one hour, at an Atlanta studio offering a twenty-dollar Tuesday promotion. Early in 2019, he began creating memes to promote the song on the microplatform video-sharing app TikTok. Part of TikTok's business model is to encourage its 500 million users to engage in "endless imitation," creating a frantic churn of content. Lil Nas X estimates that he made around one hundred memes to promote the song and created a "#Yeehaw Challenge": millions of users posted videos of themselves dressed as cowgirls or wranglers, using the song as their soundtrack. By July 2019, these videos had been viewed more than 67 million times. "Old Town Road" was diamond certified by November of the same year, reached number one on the US Billboard Hot 100, and remained at the top for nineteen weeks—the longest for any song since the chart debuted in 1958.

"The record companies have to figure out where they fit," Jimmy told us. "Right now, they are just looking for artists who are [the] most popular and paying them the most money. But that doesn't scale. Young artists are very sophisticated and have very sophisticated partners, and the more they learn about how to leverage technology, the more sophisticated they get. The artists are going to win."

World Records and Golden Records

In Chapter 3, we talked about how collaboration can build community among artists. As Madame Gandhi said, the same thing can happen when artists connect with fans. Let's return to Live Aid for a moment. In 1984, the songwriter Bob Geldof traveled to Africa after hearing a report of a famine that killed hundreds of thousands of Ethiopians. In response to the suffering he saw, he returned to London and called together the most famous pop artists in England and Ireland to record a single to benefit relief efforts. "Do They Know It's Christmas?" was recorded by an ensemble including Culture Club, Duran Duran, Phil Collins, U2, and Wham! In America, Michael Jackson and Lionel Richie heard the song and were inspired to write "We Are the World"— which was recorded by the pair, along with fellow artists including Harry Belafonte, Bob Dylan, Cyndi Lauper, Paul Simon, Bruce

Springsteen, Tina Turner, and Stevie Wonder. Taken together, the two singles raised more than $50 million.

The Live Aid concert was an extension of these fundraising efforts, founded by Geldof and performed for 72,000 fans at Wembley Stadium with 100,000 more gathered at Philadelphia's JFK Stadium and beamed live around the world, raising $127 million. The show set a world record for largest simultaneous rock concert television audience: 1.9 billion people in 150 countries. But it wasn't really about setting records. The show created lifelong fans for the bands and raised money to keep people from starving. It also shaped a community united around a mission. It wasn't just about having a good idea and a good cause—the performance made this possible. The bands used their musical talents to emphasize compassion and empathy, qualities that make us uniquely human and build connection with others.

Just how far can we take this idea? In 1977, NASA launched the *Voyager 1* spacecraft toward the stars to collect data about the outer reaches of our solar system. But the rocket had a secondary mission: in its cargo bay are two copper records, plated in gold. The contents of these records, curated by Carl Sagan, include pictures of life on earth, along with more than one hundred tracks of sounds: natural phenomena like thunderstorms, erupting volcanoes, and a baby crying; greetings in fifty-five languages; and a twenty-seven-song musical playlist that ranges from Beethoven to Chuck Berry. Along with the records is a wordless etched diagram in binary code, with instructions on how to play them. NASA was looking to connect through sight and sound with any intelligent life-forms that might be out there.

This cosmic mixtape never saw public release until 2017, when graphic designer Lawrence Azerrad teamed up with David Pescovitz, a research director at the Institute for the Future, and Timothy Daly, a manager at Amoeba Music in San Francisco. The trio reproduced the ninety-minute playlist on three translucent gold vinyl LPs, along with a hardbound book of the images, a digital download card for the audio, and a lithograph of the original cover diagram. Launched on Kickstarter, the project blew through its $180,000 goal to raise a total of $1.36 million and won a Grammy Award. In other words, it turns out that not just aliens but Earthlings were drawn to the project and the connection it offered.

When we talked to Lawrence from his sunny Los Angeles studio, he seemed pleased but not surprised. As the designer of iconic album sleeves for Esperanza Spalding, the Red Hot Chili Peppers, Sting, and others, he knows how to connect with audiences.

"The *Voyager* record is not an album you chill out to, you know?" he said. "It's highly esoteric. I wonder how many people have actually listened to it end to end. But people wanted the artifact, this touchstone in history, and what it represented."

At the time of our conversation, Lawrence had just finished designing the album artwork for Wilco's eleventh studio album, *Ode to Joy*. The two projects might not seem to have a lot of overlap, but for Lawrence, both are about creating authentic connections.

"As a graphic designer, I had to learn how to get myself out of the way of the musicians' message. It's not about my art; it's about their art. And then when it goes out into the public, it becomes the public's art. They take ownership and possession of it. I think of the cover of *Yankee Hotel Foxtrot* [Wilco's fourth album, which he also designed]. It's a very straightforward album cover, but people tie it to the experiences that they had when they were listening to it. And that, I think, is where covers become so important. *Abbey Road* means something to so many people because that record marked a turning point in culture, a coalescence in the zeitgeist."

When working with Jeff Tweedy on *Ode to Joy*, Lawrence was asked to create an accompanying pop-up book that embraced the idea of nothingness. Lawrence joked that since the idea of a white album had already been taken, they looked for other ways to connect with fans through the graphics. His illustrations echo the rhythm of the songs; Wilco's lyrics are treated as visual poetry, revealed through die-cut holes that open and close when a card shifts or a crank turns. Photographs of the band are reduced to mere silhouettes, as private and introverted as Tweedy himself. Fans know it and feel it from the moment they pick up their copy. They can sense the band in the design.

For Lawrence, design is about exploring questions of identity and the links forged between artist and audience. The desire that makes someone proud to display their favorite cover comes from the same gut-level response that a concert-goer feels wearing a Queen T-shirt or an Apple zealot feels applauding at a developer conference. It's less about losing yourself in fandom than finding yourself through believing in an artist you love and imagining with them. And that's pure as gold.

In this age of avatars that can seem more real than the people behind them, one thing seems clear: our symbols can be meaningful when authenticity is at their core. Just imagine how aliens might feel if they were to discover *Voyager*'s LPs. The vehicle for communication, the materials, the diagrams, and the format are all designed to communicate bits and pieces of who we are as humans. But even if the aliens can't crack the code to play the record, they may understand it as a desire to connect.

Feeling Connected

Not everyone has the opportunity to connect with global (or intergalactic) audiences. But if you learn to tap into the things that matter to you personally, you can communicate them with real emotion and intent.

A few months after our conversation with her, Madame Gandhi said that her goal is not to reach everyone; we can touch the people around us, no matter how big or small our circles.

"I think people believe they have to do something on a major scale," she told *Tom Tom Mag*, "but I think the most important step is asking yourself, What is your sphere of influence? Who are you interfacing with everyday? Whether it's on your social media, or it's your own community. I think it's actually way harder to try and influence your own family and friends than it is to just blindly post on social media to some audience that you don't necessarily know. I try my best to have interesting and difficult conversations with family members and friends so I can practice explaining my own values and viewpoints of the world with kindness and with empathy."

Artists want to express ideas through their craft and to relate to other people through that expression. The same is true of entrepreneurs. But this requires an awareness of your own personal strengths and a commitment to expressing what matters to you, to others. We're going to talk more about this in the final chapter of the book, but for now, we want to make one point: the wheels of our subconscious are always in motion, as an additional layer of processing information and understanding how it is relevant to our lives. As a result, some thoughts or emotions that are difficult to express in words can still be expressed in other ways. Music is certainly one example of this idea, but there are many others. A product or service can connect with people on a deeply human level. In fact, this can make the difference between an average user experience and a great one. Although this can be hard to articulate or defend in budget conversations or when allocating time and resources in corporate cultures, it's absolutely necessary in order to be successful, particularly in an information-overloaded age.

Kevin Grady is executive vice president and head of design at FCB, America's oldest advertising agency (founded in 1873!). In a previous life, he was the founder of a pop-culture publication called *Lemon*, which featured original work created with the likes of David Bowie, Daft Punk, Jeff Koons, and Sonic Youth. Hardly a typical ad agency pedigree, yet his gamble paid off: his work has won awards at Cannes, D&AD, and *The One Show*.

Kevin's two most well-known projects are the redesign of the Food and Drug Administration's nutrition facts panel or label, found on most packaged food, and a television commercial created for the Truth anti-tobacco campaign, which featured a cowboy with a tracheotomy singing through his throat to tell kids to stop smoking.

When redesigning the nutrition facts panel, commissioned as part of the Obama administration's initiative to encourage healthier eating, Kevin said, "I was picturing a mom who had a screaming baby, or an elderly person, or perhaps a diabetic person with eye issues." So he made choices that a nutritionist or packaging expert might not have, such as tripling the font size for calorie counts. After his concept for the singing cowboy was nominated for two Emmys, he said: "It won a lot of awards but more importantly really had an impact on teen smoking. What's actually been quite important to me—and the main reason I got into advertising—is things like the Truth account, to be involved in causes that I find important."

Kevin talked openly with us last fall about the importance of exploring what is personally important to you, how to draw on it to build purposeful interactions, and not being afraid of feelings.

"When I was starting out as a designer, I spent a lot of time working really hard on client projects. I still do. But there are constraints that you can't avoid. You may have an idea of the best way for something to be expressed, and the client may have a different idea. And their idea actually might be better. At a certain point, I realized I wanted to have control over something, and that's how *Lemon* was born. In it, I was free to explore whatever was obsessing me, David Bowie or whatever it was at the time, trying to make it into a theme so I could invite other people to bring their take on those obsessions. I was doing it really as a total white, pop-culture nerd geeking out [on] cool stuff; people who are like-minded tended to see that, sniff that out, and want to be a part of it."

What you feel deeply, so do others. And when they connect, it's first on that visceral level—catching your confidence, your aspiration, your mission. Kevin also explores this as a musician. Even though he doesn't play an instrument, he has an electronic music recording deal with Cleopatra Records in Los Angeles under the moniker Black Plastic.

"I come up with the melodies relatively easily. I understand structure. I have great collaborators. And in the case of music, people are either responding to it or not, they like it or they don't. [For] the people who do listen, it's like we're connecting on some nonverbal level. With Black Plastic, I knew I wanted to do dark music. It's not because I have any particular interest in goth but because I think the world can be a really dark place, and for me, music is a great way to deal with that darkness. The music might be synthesized, but the words are very real, and the emotion of it is very, very real. Hopefully, that's what gives it some kind of soul."

An early title of this chapter was "Performing." But as we wrote, we realized that performance isn't the right way to describe this. We are always performing: in our jobs, in our relationships, on the internet. But what a great performer is looking for and creating in audiences isn't about the show. It's about something much deeper: exploring what we believe, imagining together, sharing an experience. Standing at the edge of a stage, singing your heart out, and hearing other voices echo their hearts back to you.

Interlude 6

These live performances capture moments where artists create spaces of suspended disbelief, shared experiences for themselves and the crowds. The songs closing out this playlist highlight additional artists cited in the chapter.

GREETINGS FROM THE SECRETARY GENERAL OF THE
  UN, *Voyager Golden Record*
RADIO GA-GA (LIVE AID), Queen
AY-OH (LIVE AID), Queen
GLORIA (LIVE AT RED ROCKS), U2
AROUND THE WORLD/HARDER, BETTER, FASTER, STRONGER
  (LIVE), Daft Punk
NATIONAL ANTHEM (LIVE), Radiohead
NORTH AMERICAN SCUM (LIVE), LCD Soundsystem
KICKING TELEVISION (LIVE), Wilco
RAPTURE (LIVE),, Blondie
SCHOOL'S OUT (LIVE), Alice Cooper
WISH YOU WERE HERE (LIVE), Pink Floyd
BOYZ, M.I.A.
BAD HABITS, Madame Gandhi

Deep Listening: *At Folsom Prison* by Johnny Cash, recorded live inside the prison walls in January 1968. You can feel the energy and camaraderie between Cash, a man who himself had been in jail seven times, and the inmates.

seven

remixing

Between Discovering and Witnessing

They're looking for profit using a model that says: "I know this worked in the past, so that must be the way we need to go in the future." And I'm in the boardroom saying: "No, that's totally wrong. What you need is a totally new design, a remix."

—Hank Shocklee

An invention is the creation of an original product, service, or process—and the ones with the most impact happen on a rhythm of centuries. The printing press, the lightbulb, $E = mc^2$. An innovation, on the other hand, is a meaningful contribution to an existing product or service. Innovations are happening all around us right now—and most of them are clever remixes of existing components that have been reshuffled into something new:

Taxi + scheduling app + maps = Uber

Radio + library of songs + app player = Spotify

Croissant + doughnut + deep fryer = the world-famous Cronut

In the music industry, remixing begins by capturing bits of sound called samples and using them to construct new beats, textures, or phrases in songs. The artist is both curator and creator, surveying other musicians' work and borrowing the pieces that interest her. And while people often think of sampling as primarily associated with hip-hop, the practice actually came to pop music through the Beatles.

Come Together, Right Now

After they retired from playing live shows in 1966, the four lads from Liverpool began experimenting with new sounds. George Harrison had brought a sitar to the studio, along with influences from time he spent in India, and was championing minimal harmonic deviations from the single C chord. And George Martin brought a tape recorder with its erase head removed. By spooling a loop of tape through the machine, the tapes automatically overdubbed and got saturated with sound. The band was curious and created more than thirty loops to play with, turning the speed up and down and reversing the tapes. For the song "Tomorrow Never Knows" from the album *Revolver*, they overdubbed samples from these tapes.

Five loops are audible in the song: a recording of McCartney's laughter, sped up to sound like seagulls; a electromechanical keyboard called a Mellotron playing on its flute setting; a Mellotron strings sound, alternating between B flat and C; an orchestral chord of B flat major; and a sped-up sitar playing a phrase from a rising scale.

Martin described the process in his book *Summer of Love: The Making of Sgt. Pepper*. The loops were played in several different studios, each one controlled by a technician who had to hold a pencil in the loop to keep tension on the tape, as the Beatles worked the faders on the mixing console. Eight tapes were used simultaneously, changed halfway through the song. Martin said that the finished mix was utterly unique and could never be repeated because of the random way that they were overdubbed on the music.

Paul McCartney says of the experience: "We played the faders, and just before you could tell it was a loop, before it began to repeat a lot, I'd pull in one of the other faders, and so . . . we did a half random, half orchestrated playing of the things and recorded that to a track on the actual master tape, so that if we got a good one, that would be the solo. We played it through a few times and changed some of the tapes till we got what we thought was a real good one."

In an interview that year, Harrison called the song "easily the most amazing new thing we've ever come up with," but also said that if audiences didn't listen with open ears, it might strike them as "a terrible mess of a sound." When McCartney played the song for Bob Dylan, he famously said, "Oh, I get it. You don't want to be cute anymore" and walked out of the room. But four decades later, this sample-based pop song has staying power: *Rolling Stone* named it number eighteen in their list of best songs by the band, and *Q* magazine placed it as the seventy-fifth greatest song of all time.

Mix and Match

The Beatles' early sampling produced a classic, but when it comes to modern sampling, Hank Shocklee is king. We introduced him in Chapter 5; our conversation with him went well beyond producing—covering sampling, remixing, and how inspiration takes shape under his hands.

Hank is known for blending rap, rock, and punk music. He is also known for his innovative, raucous, atonal, and multilayered "walls of noise" that turned sampling into art, often incorporating dozens of samples on just one track.

"First of all, you have to understand something. I'm more of a film person than I am a music person," he told us. "Everything for me starts with an idea or story, and that goes for music too. Music has to have an idea."

Hank's mother was a concert pianist who taught him music theory, and for him, the theory is what creates the application. We asked him if, when writing songs, he thinks of the story first or a mood and a feeling—and how he starts to pull from different sources to build the story he is trying to create.

"It's like reverse engineering. Start with an idea, then the idea takes you to what you need to look for in terms of other ideas and samples. Everything has to give you a mood. I don't look at music in terms of the actual instruments, the bass or drums or synth or guitars. The only thing that matters is frequency. With frequency, you get color."

Hank is not talking about synesthesia, a condition that Kanye West, Stevie Wonder, Mary J. Blige, Lorde, Pharrell Williams, and many other musicians have, where musical notes trigger a color in their visual field or a flavor on their tongue. He is talking about something deeper, rooted in feeling, that is accessible to anyone.

"If you look at the visual spectrum and the audio spectrum, they mirror each other. They have the same frequencies. So the idea is to try to mix and match the frequency to invoke a certain feeling you want to get. People ask me: 'How do you come up with these samples, what made you decide to pick them?' It's not so much what made us choose one over another; it's the feeling that the sample or particular sound represents. What does a sound communicate? And does it communicate on a three-dimensional level? That's how a particular sound makes it onto a particular project."

When he described the first steps of this process, it reminded us of Desmond Child working with Bob Crewe, tossing song titles at each other. "We would start with an outline, me and Chuck D would sit down and just put titles up on the board. Lots and lots of different titles. Then we'd look at those titles and find the central theme that they had in common. From there, we started to narrow down into exactly what the project would be and what it was going to communicate."

We asked him if it works both ways, where he starts with an image or idea as a jumping-off point, and he answered with an emphatic no.

"I've never done anything from that perspective, where you have an idea and try to find something to fit that idea. I find that to be problematic because it locks you in a certain phase. And I don't want to be locked into any phase," he said. "The vibrations are the thing that I go for first. I let the vibrations tell the story. But you have to be in tune to a lot of things at the same time. You've got to be in tune to your environment; you've got to be in tune to what's happening around you, what's happening on the street level, in current events and historical events. You have to tap into all of those energies and channel them. And then the frequencies that you're looking for will come to you."

To be able to accomplish this at a high level, Hank believes that you have to know your craft inside and out, as well as every piece of equipment—both what it can do and its limitations. But the limitations of equipment are not an obstacle or a stopping point; they are an invitation to expand what the equipment can do.

"It's funny because when I get a new piece of gear, I spend an enormous amount of time in the laboratory or in your research and development phase. It's a slow process. You don't just come up with greatness overnight. It's not poppin' fresh; it doesn't work that way. I learn every piece of gear backward and forward, and then I know what I can do to use it in any way possible or not. It's true of yourself, too. Don't worry about trying to be that musician you admire; just be the greatest you. Know your strengths and your weaknesses."

Hank also applied this methodology to working with bands and collaborators. He might cut and splice and remix samples, but when it came to people, he was more interested in managing the environment than the person.

"As a producer, we don't get the luxury to pick who we want to work with all the time, all right? Most of the time, you're being thrown artists who are not very good. And their thing is: 'Well, you're a hit maker, so I want you to make a hit for my artist.' Wrong. That doesn't work. My reference is going to be: What can I do with this artist that's different from what's already out there, and different from what the artist has already been doing? How do I leverage and/or conceal his strengths and weaknesses?"

You can remix talent, too. He told a remarkable story about the three members of R&B powerhouse New Edition who, in 1989, left the group after Bobby Brown's departure. Hank was asked to work with three of the group's backup singers: Ricky Bell, Michael Bivins, and Ronnie DeVoe. The challenge? None of them sang lead vocals.

"My first thought was: Why can't I get Bobby Brown, Ralph Tresvant, or Johnny Gill? You want the lead, but sometimes you don't have that opportunity. So the first thing I do is ask these guys: OK, what are your strengths and weaknesses? Ricky Bell, that guy can hold a note. He can hold the harmonies. Michael and Ronnie were more like background singers. They needed to have someone be the lead, and then they could fill in the gaps."

Hank approached the challenge as a remix project: he asked Michael and Ronnie to rap and for Ricky to focus on singing vocals. It worked. They became Bell Biv DeVoe, and two singles from their debut album both reached number three on the Billboard Hot 100. Taking advantage of each person's strengths enabled the band to nearly outsell New Edition.

Another example of remixing, with even higher stakes, came when he worked with rapper and producer Ice Cube on his debut studio album, *AmeriKKKa's Most Wanted*. At the time in 1990, the East and West Coasts bred very different styles. The East Coast sound was rapid, almost combative; the West was more melodic.

"They were basically two different planets. Back in the day, the East Coast artists weren't really feeling the West Coast artists, and vice versa. We brought a prominent artist from the West Coast and brought him to make an authentic record with his sound, but at the same with the sensitivities of the East Coast. How did we manage that, where both were vibing on the same record, and to build a bridge between the two?

"That's intelligent design. That's when it all comes together. And you can only do that by tapping into the frequencies, a third dimension."

One thing we heard over and over again from Hank was that everything he needs to create something new is already at hand. But if you are unable to tap into the frequencies, you're going to choose the wrong things. Or you'll end up with a product nearly identical to your source material. And Hank has consistently disrupted and innovated, not only in music but in business.

"My schooling is in economics; I never went to school for music. But I saw very quickly that the creative world doesn't understand the business world, and the business never understands the creative. So there's always this friction. Music is about no deadlines, no time lines, let me be free flowing with my idea, let me connect to this vast universe of resources to create a particular piece. Whereas the business world is the opposite: deadlines, punctuation, and numbers. I've been able to speak both languages to the musician and to the executive.

"You have to know what business is looking for. Profit. But most of the time they're looking for profit using a model that says: 'I know this worked in the past, so that must be the way we need to go in the future.' And I'm in the boardroom saying: 'No, that's totally wrong. What you're looking for is a totally new design, a remix.' It's like taking a machine that was meant to do one thing, and I'm saying: 'No, I don't want that machine to do what you say it can do. I want to do something totally different with it, but I want to get to the same place.' This is how you come up with new concepts and new ideas. We have all the tools today, but we're not remixing them enough. We're not getting inside; we're not being creative enough."

When opportunities present themselves, a story or a mood or a way to connect with deeper vibrations, Hank does more than draw on a mental library. He deliberately makes the choice to stay open, to receive, with empathy.

"What keeps me humble is that I'm in awe of everything. I'm a fan of everything. I want to know what you're feeling, and to be a good producer you almost have to go out of body and get into the artist or project that you're producing. This is how I make that connection—looking at things from an outside perspective so I can see what other people are going through. Then I can use that energy to help me manifest an idea that I'm trying to get across, and it becomes more honest and more sincere."

That Synth Sound

Remixing, or synthesizing, is a musician's skill and an entrepreneur's necessity. The ability to take disparate information, identify the connections and patterns, and turn those various elements into a unified whole is how inventions and innovations are made. Apple's first mouse appropriated a deodorant roller ball into the user interface. Pay at the pump convenience of gas stations combine ATM interfaces with field dispensers.

When we talk about synthesizers, you might picture a Yamaha electric keyboard onstage or in your grandmother's basement. The first synthesizer was a combination of electronic sound generators and sequencers created by French inventors Edouard Coupleux and Joseph Givelet in 1929. According to their US patent application, the duo named their creation the "automatically operating musical instrument of the electric oscillation type." Because the AOMIOTEOT was too hard to remember or pronounce, most people simply called it the Coupleux-Givelet synthesizer. Its engineering was simple in concept but intricate in execution, marrying electronic sound to a mechanically punched tape control. The term *synthesizer* was picked up in 1956 by RCA Electronics for their Mark I punch card model, developed by American engineers Harry F. Olson and Herbert Belar. But synthesizers as we know them today came into their own as musical instruments in the 1960s through the innovative work of a guy named Bob Moog.

The 1960s were a time of intense experimentation—in art forms, in communal living, with psychedelic drugs, with new forms of religion. People everywhere were mentally separating from their historical biases and assumptions, committed to thinking freely, and every corner of culture was opened up to exploration, adaptation, and re-creation.

Moog was the son of an engineer and a physics major. As a teenager, he fell in love with an electronic instrument called the theremin, which looks like a small wooden radio with an oversized antenna and is best known for creating the eerie, ethereal sound effects of early science-fiction and horror movies. An unwieldy instrument, it is hard to control and almost impossible to master.

As an adult, Moog owned a music shop in upstate New York, and when musicians visited, he would give them a short theremin lesson. One day Brian Wilson of the Beach Boys came into the shop. Moog showed him how to play it (you might have noticed its appearance on a little song called "Good Vibrations"). Wilson played around with it and told Moog that if a theremin were ever going to be viable for pop music, it needed frets like a guitar.

Beginning in the late 1950s, Moog experimented with all kinds of materials in a makeshift laboratory, finally landing on a long stretch of ribbon salvaged from a 1920s machine, with markers showing where to place your hand to create a certain musical note. Then, in 1963, Moog met the composer Herbert Deutsch, who inspired him to combine a voltage-controlled oscillator and amplifier module with a keyboard. The result was the first prototype of a voltage-controlled synthesizer—an instrument that makes music entirely from sound frequencies.

With the keyboard in place, Moog still had to create the different sounds or modules that it could make: piano, cello, thunderclap. The possibilities were endless. All he had to do was play with the tones and experiment with manipulating them until they sounded right.

In the award-winning documentary *Moog: A Documentary Film*, he says: "It would be egotistical of me to say, 'I thought of it,' what happened is, I opened my mind and the idea came through me. . . . It's something between discovering and witnessing."

As Moog discovered, others did too. One pair of synth sojourners was Alan Pearlman and David Friend, who cofounded ARP Instruments in 1969 and quickly won fans from the likes of Stevie Wonder, the Who, and Led Zeppelin. David, now the CEO of hot cloud storage start-up Wasabi, studied composition at Yale, but after graduating, he felt that he wouldn't make a satisfactory living, so he went to grad school in electrical engineering.

"I have always been a tech geek anyway—ham radio as a kid, always building electronic stuff. Turns out, I have discovered that starting companies has much the same feel as composition: in both cases you are, at least metaphorically, starting with a blank sheet of paper."

David explained that when he started ARP, synthesizers were new to the world and no one really knew how they would be used. There was a thrill in hearing different performers play them. "Listening to what Stevie Wonder did with a 2600 or Herbie Hancock did with an Odyssey was always amazing to us. Stevie Wonder got his first synthesizer lesson in my office," he shared nonchalantly. But beyond just a range of new-to-the-world sounds, there were also questions about usability. Synthesizers were like studio gear—heavy, fragile electronic furniture not designed or engineered for the ease of use, durability, and mobility required for stage performance. Even more specifically, musicians struggled with patch cords, the cables that connect inputs and outputs, ranging from electrical control to audio, in a modular synthesizer. There are often so many on the instrument that it looks like it's covered in multicolored spaghetti. Though no one had asked him to address this, he saw it as an issue and took action.

"When I saw 2600 users struggling onstage with patch cords, I said, 'We have to get rid of *all* patch cords,' something that had never been done before," he continued. "No musicians had ever asked for a synthesizer with no patch cords because they probably couldn't envision how you could do it, but that's what invention is all about." This ability to see the whole picture—the context, the technology, and the user—identify the common needs, and then anticipate what should be done next has informed all seven of the start-ups David has founded since his early days at ARP Instruments.

"Many business execs believe that if you just listen to your customers and let them tell you what they need, you'll succeed. I don't believe that's true. If all you do is make what customers say they want, it's like driving by looking in the rearview mirror. You have to create something that is beyond what most people can see. If everybody already sees it, then it's too late." Like David, like Hank, you have to tap into the frequencies.

Somewhere Between Discovering and Witnessing

The Beatles, Hank Shocklee, and Bob Moog are all examples of people who worked through their process of remixing with a spirit of open discovery, empathy, and craft. As a result, a single, collective perspective emerges—without any one voice stronger than the others. We have both seen this in our professional lives, both in our backgrounds as entrepreneurs and, more recently, in collaborations between our respective companies and partners in the United Arab Emirates. Panos launched Berklee Abu Dhabi; Michael's colleagues developed a creative lab called Palmwood in Dubai, a mash-up of IDEO and the United Arab Emirates (UAE) government ministries. In each case, the partnerships are united by a shared purpose, sampling from Middle Eastern and Western cultures to create something entirely new.

When Berklee was founded in 1945, it was the first music school in the world built upon a curriculum of teaching contemporary music—the music of the day. Traditional conservatories scoffed at an upstart program that wanted to teach jazz theory and performance in an academic setting, but the idea was both revolutionary and timely: GIs were returning from World War II hoping to find work in jazz bands but without many prospects. Four years later, the college had more than five hundred students.

In the years since, Berklee has continued to push the boundaries of what contemporary music education means, becoming the first institution to embrace the electric guitar as an instrument; the first to introduce majors in sound design, songwriting, and film scoring; the first to include synthesizers, turntables, and electronic digital modules as instruments. For the faculty, the goal has always been to open doors and opportunities that are relevant to the moment. This pursuit of relevance has led us to forge new connections among art forms, musical traditions, technologies, and institutions, creating a global network that pursues innovation, collaboration, and community. In 2018, with established campuses, institutes, and centers in Boston, New York, and Valencia, Spain, we set our sights on the Middle East.

After all, if our goal is to create an interconnected educational community that supports new artistic expressions that bring formerly disconnected people together, how could we ignore Arabic countries and Middle Eastern culture?

From the beginning of his conversations with the Department of Culture and Tourism in Abu Dhabi, Panos met with its chairman, Mohamed Khalifa Al Mubarak. Born in Abu Dhabi and educated at Boston's Northeastern University, where he majored in economics and political science, Al Mubarak has been responsible for education projects, fostering the film industry in the country, and shaping the urban fabric through iconic real estate developments—reporting directly to Sheikh Mohammed bin Zayed Al Nahyan, the son of Abu Dhabi's crown prince.

Panos knew that the Department of Culture had already brought satellites of the Louvre and Guggenheim Museums, New York University, and a performing arts center designed by Zaha Hadid to the Saadiyat Island Cultural District. The country had already invested in a 42,000-square-foot pavilion for the Shanghai 2010 Expo—dismantling all twenty-four thousand stainless steel pieces for a four-thousand-mile voyage before they were reconstructed on site. But it was only the shell of a building, and the department was looking to partner with organizations who could help train Abu Dhabi's young people in music, dance, and theater. Their choice to team up with Berklee came down to the fact that the UAE government's objective is to build creative capacity among its young people. While other schools might insist that dance, music, and theater are performance disciplines grounded in orthodox interpretations of other people's music, Berklee was forward looking, believing that the arts enable contemporary creative expressions that have not even been written yet.

This perspective connected with the leaders of Abu Dhabi. The Emiratis could see that Berklee was not trying to impose a Western way of teaching music, teaching students to perform other people's work. Rather, we want to build upon what is already there, to work with young Arabs as they find their own next creative expression, and then share it with the world. It helped tremendously that we have a history of doing this kind of work with alumni from throughout the Middle East and North Africa region. Just one such example: Pinar Toprak, a Turkish American Berklee grad, is a composer for film, television, and video games. In addition to receiving two International Film Music Critics Association Awards, she recently scored the blockbuster movie *Captain Marvel*—the first woman composer ever to land a billion-dollar superhero movie.

It was April 2019, and the Department of Culture and Tourism's executive director, Rita Abdo Aoun, said: "Can you move fast enough to have the center ready by early 2020?" Panos's reply was both persuasive and true: "If you can build it out, I guarantee we can do our part."

In January of 2020, a month before the center opened, Panos toured the site. The building had been transformed, outfitted with performance spaces, a recording studio, rehearsal studios, practice rooms, ensemble rooms, and a multimedia technology lab. On this trip, Panos met with both Mohamed Al Mubarak and Sheikh Mohammed bin Zayed. He was surprised and delighted at how soft spoken and attuned to listening closely the sheikh is, how he is a man who has no need of pretense—even his sandals were humble and functional underneath his robes. Here is a man who is committed to furthering the vision of his grandfather, the founder of the UAE, whose fifty-year strategy, established before oil was discovered in the country, has used culture as a means of education to transform a group of Bedouins into the thriving epicenter that the country is today.

As they talked, the sheikh asked questions about music for young children, how it can shape the lives of young people. At one point in the conversation, Mohamed Al Mubarak pulled out his mobile phone to show a video of his twin daughters singing Idina Menzel's hit song "Let It Go" from the Disney movie *Frozen*. As it turns out, Panos has twin daughters too—and we're not ashamed to admit that Panos knows every word of the song! There we were: three people from different backgrounds, experiences, and cultures, yet our daughters all express themselves in the same way—through a shared favorite song.

A month later, on the night of the opening of Berklee Abu Dhabi, we all attended the opening concert. It was a sight to behold: the band onstage included Emirati, Lebanese, Indian, Jordanian, Mexican, French, American, and Japanese musicians, as well as Steve Vai, the legendary guitar hero and inventor you met earlier. An amazing mixture of people and cultures, all singing from the same songbook, to encourage the young people in the audience to write their own.

One of our favorite moments came later in the weekend. We have a wonderful photograph of our friend and colleague Stephen Webber, executive director of Berklee New York City, teaching a turntable class. Around the table are gathered a remarkable mix of women wearing Indian saris, Western garb, and hijabs. It struck us: for many young people in Abu Dhabi, this will be the first time that they are able to express their experiences and tell their stories through the arts and put them out into the world. For millennia, many women have never had a chance to lend their voices and express their unique experiences, which have grown out of their daily lives. Through music, technology, and culture, they will be able to share something new and wonderful with the world.

IDEO has recently had a parallel experience in the UAE. In recent years, more and more of IDEO's clients have come to the company seeking to collaborate on projects—a significant shift from the company's project-based roots, in which a client would present a challenge for IDEO to solve. In response IDEO has created labs that form integrated design teams composed of staff from both IDEO and the client. These are mash-ups, such as Ford and IDEO; Mitsui and IDEO; and Target, MIT, and IDEO. The firm has always believed in open communication and inclusion, and this was the next logical step.

Like Berklee, IDEO's work in the UAE is a collaboration with the government, based in Dubai. The creative organization Palm-wood began with the vision of Mohammad Abdullah Gergawi, who is the chairman of the Executive Office of His Highness Sheikh Mohammed bin Rashid Al Maktoum and the minister of Cabinet Affairs and the Future of the United Arab Emirates. His titles alone are an indication of the responsibility he carries and the respect he has earned.

At the World Government Summit in 2016, Gergawi said from the stage: "We live in a tough neighborhood. Radicalism and extremism are on our doorstep. We need to counteract this radicalism with radical new forms of creativity."

Palmwood is an incarnation of this vision, building the future of the UAE around a core question: What would happen if we took the ideas of teenagers seriously, helping to build their creative muscles? The initiative designs the intersection of government projects focused on making the UAE the most creative nation in the world by fostering community conversations and empowering businesses, artists, and entrepreneurs to build the creative economy of the future. The organization was established to amplify the ever-renewable resources of curiosity, generosity, and creativity in the Arab people. From the day that Palmwood opened its doors, the UAE and IDEO have tackled challenges of food security, education, ageism, and mental health together, resulting in the creation of new programs and policies in the country. It is an experiment in radical collaboration between two completely different cultures, two completely different mindsets: one government, the other designers; one the Middle East, the other California, which is the birthplace of counterculture and, as luck would have it, of IDEO. We wanted to know what would happen if we created a remix with the magic of California optimism and Middle Eastern audacity and carried those together to take on redesigning an entire nation.

When Michael first visited Dubai, he was struck by the mosaic of cultural influences. There was the obvious: desert, heat, sand, and spitting camels—all new to someone who grew up in Tennessee. But it was also a high-tech city formed by iconic architecture, new highways, and electric cars. Mosques sit in the shadow of the Burj Khalifa, which comes alive nightly with a laser light show. Security robots greet shoppers as they enter the mall to view sharks and whales in a massive aquarium among the luxury stores. It was clear that it's a culture already embracing the remix.

A transplant from Michael's Cambridge studio, Mitch Sinclair is chief creative officer of Palmwood and an executive design director at IDEO. In Dubai, you can often see her in a contrasting black-and-white sheath dress, wearing bright red lipstick. She's bold inside and out. When we asked her about this remix culture within Palmwood, how it felt to have a team composed of IDEO-ers and government employees with completely different backgrounds, Mitch lit up:

"I think one thing that drew us to each other was a shared sense of restlessness," she said. "Bedouin culture was born from living in the shifting sands. Every morning you wake up in dunes that have a different shape from the day before, that are literally in a different place. There's a similar mindset in designers: 'I don't know what's next, let's experiment, let's try it, let's do something new.' The cool thing was there's a lot that we share, but we didn't blend it together into a muddy gray. We said: 'You do you and we'll do us, and we'll figure out this new thing in between.' It's not a gradient. There was a recognition that we were coming in with a lot to teach but also with a lot to learn. There's a humility in it."

One project, undertaken in 2019, illustrates how this remix mindset has played out. Like all the initiatives adopted by Palmwood, their mission was cocreated: the initial idea was to create an alternative story to radicalism that shines a light on the positivity and beauty of the Islamic faith. But as we tested this idea with young Muslims, they challenged it.

We were told that "what you need to get at is the root of separation and the bubbles across society that keep us apart. Everyone lives in their own insular worlds—Christians fear Muslims, Sunni are separate from Shia, liberals fight conservatives, nations retreat to their own worlds, and the next generation of youth is trying to navigate their identity and faith in a world that's both more connected and more isolated than ever."

This reminded Mitch of the edge effect, an idea that the renowned cellist Yo-Yo Ma wrote into the mission for his nonprofit arts organization the Silkroad (formerly the Silk Road Project). Inspired by the edge effect in ecosystems—where, for example, forest meets field, creating a new habitat—the edge effect in art works to bring together the best of different cultures to create a new one in the overlap. Yo-Yo does this with music, and Mitch thought that it might extend to other creative expressions.

To get started, the Palmwood team hosted a series of dinner parties that brought together unexpected combinations of people: for example, a Muslim woman with her teenage daughter and her grandmother, a Christian American, an Emirati government leader, an artist, and a rabbi. The diners were asked questions around identity, faith, and belonging, topics that people in the UAE do not often talk about beyond their own circles. Each event quickly took on a life of its own and ended with guests exchanging contact information so they could cohost their own dinners. Mitch showed us a photograph from one of these organic follow-up gatherings: five young women—Emirati, Israeli, Kenyan, American, and Japanese—are seated around a small apartment table, vulnerably discussing faith and identity, sharing their stories, finding common ground.

It was clear that a new space needed to be created, not only for dialogue but also for cocreation, to mix—or remix—these different ideas. The concept of a foundation established to host this kind of mash-up emerged, and Mitch, along with her IDEO collaborators, assembled a team to develop it.

"We knew from the beginning that designers from California and Boston could not own the visual language of this foundation. They only represent one point of view, and that would be super disrespectful to the locals," Mitch explained. "So we set up a variety of collaborators. One was a young Emirati photographer. We also worked with a Saudi material designer and Rapapawn, a video production house in Spain. We asked them to create something that would speak to global youth in a language that did not feel like a government or a formal 'interfaith' effort. In the 080 brand, you can feel a raw, edgy, global, youthful style, born of the Middle East but not just for the Middle East. It's a gift from the Arabic world to the rest of the world, saying, 'Hey, this is another way we can all be.'"

As the scope grew, the team did too, bringing in a Jordanian Canadian architect, a Turkish design researcher, a graphic designer from Minnesota, a first-generation Indian American business designer, and a Syrian copywriter. The team was already embodying the mandate of the newly forming foundation, bringing together the edges of Arabic and Western design to shape a new culture.

Mitch also shared a moment from her research with an interfaith arts community called Sanctuaries.

"When two people with different beliefs come toward each other, there is too often a posture of 'against.' But when you are creating something with another person, there's a posture of 'forward' because you are side by side. Rather than just talking, we're making something together, we're creating a new product, we're creating a new service. It feels like the energy is focused in a shared direction."

When you look at Palmwood, or the work of the 080 Foundation, it's impossible to discern a single author. That's the beauty of the remix. It's a synthesis of sources brought seamlessly together to create a new whole. Like a song, the individual parts may be identified, but unless it's heard with others, it is incomplete.

Finding Mutual Coordinates

Earlier, we shared how Björk's close listening for emotional connections helped her investment company and her country during the 2008 financial crisis. As it turns out, the Icelandic singer has also brought to education her unique vision of how music, nature, and technology intersect. Collaborating with scientists, app developers, writers, inventors, instrument makers, and other musicians, she created the Biophilia Educational Project, a unique multimedia exploration of the universe and its physical forces, from the atomic to the cosmic.

The initiative is named after her 2011 album *Biophilia*, which was released as a multimedia project, including a studio album, an app album for iPad, a live tour, and educational workshops. The lyrics of each of the album's ten songs dwell on a scientific theme. For example, "Crystalline" draws on the structural complexity of crystals, an idea mirrored in the instrumentation; "Virus" multiplies and repeats phrases.

"For me, lines blur so easily between music and nature because they're almost the same thing for me," she said. "The project is about the sound of sound and celebrating how it works in nature."

The app component of the project is made up of ten modules, each one built around one of the songs on the album. Each module takes a bit of music theory—chords, scales, arpeggios, counterpoint, and so on—and relates it to a scientific phenomenon. The goal is to decomplexify music theory by relating it to simple, familiar, natural experiences.

In developing the app, she worked with sound engineers around a central question: How easy is the interface to use? Does it integrate seamlessly with the software? Ultimately, the team decided to go with a technology that was not only proven but also familiar to young students: the touchscreen. Using their hands, users fly past planets named after the songs, watch the score render on scrolling sheet music, or interact with the song itself by bending notes, clicking for more content or learning, and even writing songs.

"Virus" is a song about a virus who loves a cell so much she destroys him. In the interactive game, users swipe invading pathogens away from the cell, but the game must be lost to be won; you cannot hear the entire song without letting the cell die. In the app for "Thunderbolt," which teaches about arpeggios, there is a bass line that you can make even more jagged by tapping or swiping on lightning icons.

While on tour, the musicians and crew held educational workshops at local art centers in the cities where they played. They wanted to connect with children between the ages of ten and twelve, in particular, to help them develop their musical imaginations, be creative in unfettered and responsible ways, and be inspired by the natural world. To Björk, the album was an opportunity to teach kids at least one song a day. "The first half of the day, they get physical artifacts: they can touch them and play with them and hear about them from a biologist. They can use the app, and the music teacher will teach them about structure in music. And then they can write their own song and take it home on a USB."

"I was trying to mix together the most exciting of electronics, where you can use cutting-edge technology to do more impulsive right brain sort of stuff for kids, but then you could plug it into the most famous acoustic instruments that man has made," she said, then added: "Hopefully, we can expand this educational side."

In an effort to expand, in 2013 Björk launched a Kickstarter campaign to fund the development of the app for Android. The Kickstarter page emphasized the app's potential for transforming education, as well as its effectiveness for students with ADHD. The goal was to raise $436,057 in thirty days, but after two weeks, the campaign had raised only 4 percent of its goal. Björk also learned that programming the app was more complicated than they had realized; it would take eight programmers five months to accomplish. So she canceled the campaign.

In a handwritten note posted to the campaign page, she said: "I cannot leave this project before this has been done, since it seems to [be] the area where it can bloom the most . . . so incredibly many have reached out to us so eager to adapt Biophilia's musicology angle to their schools."

In fact, only six months later the app was complete. She had found a mobile technology partner that was able to port the iOS app to Android.

"They came up with a new way of converting apps to Android that costs a whole lot less and takes far less time than previously expected," explained a blog post on Björk's website. "Luckily for us, technology had developed so now it is possible to do this at a fraction of the cost."

The project has since spread to multiple Nordic countries, including Greenland and the Faroe Islands. Under the supervision of Reykjavik grade-school teachers, scientists from the University of Iceland, and the Nordic Council of Ministers, students learn musical composition and collaboration and how to develop their own creativity. In many ways, the project has the same objectives of STEAM curricula in the United States: programs that emphasize learning in science, technology, engineering, arts, and math. But the seamlessness and creativity of the Biophilia Educational Project make it stand out. This remix of subjects, using tools typically not available to schools, continues to grow; it is a dynamic collaboration among school systems, cultural institutions, and institutes of science and research. Björk's apps are now a standard part of music education curricula in Iceland and have spread beyond Nordic countries: the curriculum, workshops, and programs are in use in Paris, São Paulo, Buenos Aires, Manchester, Los Angeles, and San Francisco.

And at the center of it all is music making.

While announcing the launch of Biophilia programs with the library and the Children's Museum of Manhattan, Björk said:

> I went to music school myself in Iceland from age five to fifteen, and I enjoyed it very much, but I was also a little frustrated. When people are teaching music it was always a very academic thing. You sit down in a chair and you're still, and somebody talks to you and you write down little points for an hour and a half, twice a week. And then you go home. For me it seemed so strange. . . . So much importance was put into learning to play the violin or the piano, being a performer, but there was no importance put into you writing music.

In the apps, the unity of technology and nature were ways not only to help children understand music theory but also to create. Each app has both song modes and instrument modes, so students can not only remix Björk's songs but also write their own. For Björk, remixing and creativity are inextricably entwined.

"To me, the word *remix* is so underestimated," she said in a 1997 interview. "Probably because until now it's been a record company's way to try to make a song more radio friendly or more successful commercially. A lot of the remixers have been incredibly creative over the years. . . . If I may, I'd like to make a comparison with this to Bach; it's similar to the organ piece he did. He didn't even write all the notes out so whoever played them had the liberty of changing it."

Interlude 7

This mix starts with three songs produced by the Bomb Squad and then moves on to tracks that showcase maximal sampling. It ends with tunes that also sample, but where the musicians seamlessly incorporated found material, so the samples disappear. We close with an amazing synthesizer collaboration. Of all the playlists in our book, this one was the hardest to create because sampling and remixing have become a defining creative process in the digital era. It was very meta: there are just so many examples of samples to draw upon!

NIGHT OF THE LIVING BASEHEADS, Public Enemy

THE BOMB, Ice Cube

BOUNCE THAT, Girl Talk

SHAKE YOUR RUMP, Beastie Boys

THE NEW POLLUTION, Beck

FLIPPED OUT, Makaya McCraven

STRONGER, Kanye West

ANGEL EYES (LAYO & BUSHWACKA! REMIX), Ella Fitzgerald

... AND THE WORLD LAUGHS WITH YOU, Flying Lotus, featuring Thom Yorke

ARCHANGEL, Burial

SHENZHOU, Biosphere

CLOSED CIRCUIT, Kaitlyn Aurelia Smith and Suzanne Ciani

Deep Listening: Here's a triple play! First check out the *Song Exploder* podcast for Björk's "Stonemilker," where she breaks down all the elements of the song. Next listen to *An Empty Bliss Beyond This World* by the Caretaker, a high concept album based on studies of Alzheimer's patients. The remix, created from scratched vintage ballroom records, deteriorates throughout the album like disappearing memories. Finally, look for *The Grey Album* by Danger Mouse, a mash-up of Jay-Z's *The Black Album* and the Beatles' *White Album*. You won't find it on streaming services.

eight
sensing

Gardening, Not Architecture

I want to rethink surrender as an active verb.

—Brian Eno

When we reconnected with Yoko Sen, she posed a question she had been asking from stages over the previous two years: "What is the last sound you want to hear before you die?" For her, it was a question of compassion, one sparked during her residency at IDEO in 2015.

Yoko was a participant in IDEO Fortnight, a two-week artist-in-residence program originated by colleague Neil Stevenson when he was editor at the British music and fashion magazine *The Face*. The concept is to bring highly creative people into your offices and give them complete freedom to respond artistically to the space in ways that will inspire employees and clients. During this residency, Yoko, an ambient electronic musician and sound artist, worked with creative technologist Ayodamola Okunseinde to create "Mother Tongue," a remarkable, beautiful sound and sculpture installation that painted an optimistic picture of the future, in which robots and people live in harmony. Yoko's soundscapes and voiceover unite with Ayo's microcomputer-powered "empathy robots" to set the stage for the primary interaction: Can robots learn how to love?

Ayo built the robot "life-forms" by injecting foam into fabric tubes; as it expanded, it leaked through the weave creating organic lumps that would look entirely at home in a Björk video. He painted these amorphous aliens and kitted them out with speakers, LED lights, and a microphone. As people spoke with them, they would "learn," responding with Yoko's pitch-manipulated voice, creating an empathy cycle. The humans care for the robots, and the robots care for the humans. As we watched the installation take shape and then learned to love the creatures (and hope they loved us back), we were unexpectedly moved. Somehow, the robots and soundscapes felt deeply personal.

As it turns out, they were. We were completely unaware that while she was in our offices, Yoko was recovering from an unexpected illness that had hospitalized her for months. She found being in the hospital dreadful not because of bad Jell-O and bedpans but because her musical mind hated the constant din of cold, inhuman alarms and beeping machines. According to a *New York Times* article, Yoko heard a cardiac monitor ring out in a tone close to the musical note of C, clashing with another device in the room that was beeping a high-pitched F sharp: a combination of notes so dissonant that medieval churches called it the devil's interval and forbade it from being played. Perhaps even worse, the sound from the machines never stopped, never reaching resolution, a state our brains crave.

"I was surrounded by all of these noises and remembered reading that hearing is your last sense to go when you die," she told us.

She realized that those beeps could be the last thing she would sense before death.

Yoko produces soothing and down-tempo music using software synthesizers, as well as by working with live musicians who play the flute, saxophone, cello, and violin. She has toured the globe performing with Rob Garza of Thievery Corporation and has twice been named the best electronic artist of Washington, DC. But her ambitions changed after she was hospitalized.

Following her time at IDEO, Yoko produced other art installations designed to provoke thinking about sound and how it contributes to (or takes away from) quality of life in health-care settings. She also heard from nurses and other practitioners who said that the sounds add to stress, not only for patients but for hospital workers. Visitors to her exhibits started asking what could be done to improve the situation.

"Suddenly, the expectation was for me to solve the problem," she told us. "I never meant to be an entrepreneur. I don't think I am one. I even don't think I'm fully qualified to be a designer. It's more like: What can I do to solve the puzzle?"

Yoko created Sen Sound, a social enterprise that aims to transform the soundscape in medical facilities. Working with Johns Hopkins Sibley Innovation Hub and Stanford Medicine X, Sen Sound is developing safer ways to alert staff to critical conditions, as well as cost-effective interventions that reduce stress not only for patients but also for nurses and doctors.

"I've had many nurses and doctors tell me that they never felt they had permission to say: 'I'm stressed out by noise,'" she told us. "We're not necessarily trying to harmonize those beeps. As a musician, that's a one-click, simple, intuitive solution. But I don't believe that is the answer. There's a small group of people who design sounds for these devices, and there are regulations that determine those sounds. The majority of people involved are not the people who have to hear those sounds as a result. I'm not saying they're bad people. I'm sure they have all the right intentions.

What we are trying to do is create a process to democratize sound design so the people who have to hear these sounds—nurses, patients, and families—are put into the center of this conversation."

As a musician, Yoko is adept at using her sense of hearing to express complex ideas. But she told us that becoming an entrepreneur opened new doors of expression and communication. "I have been an empathetic person, but I wasn't an open person," she said. "I was actually very closed up, and it was more that music was the only way I knew how to enter the world because I didn't know how to connect to people otherwise. It changed a lot these past several years because I was forced to articulate ideas and talk to different people."

"I see this shift taking place, which in many ways, are the foundations of this systemic change that hopefully we are going to see in the next couple of years," she said. "Talking about something fearful and taboo, like end of life, strips us into bare minimum humans. Our titles don't matter; our professions don't matter. It forces people to be vulnerable—but once people are willing to go [to] that place, different cultures don't matter, different ages don't matter. It has a way of connecting us. We all die. Pop media, pop culture are there to distract us because it's scary as shit. So we don't think about it. But when we face that fear, there's a beauty. It makes us live life more fully and puts things in perspective."

We're all familiar with the ways that our bodily senses come into play when we communicate. Think about a time when you were frustrated and your hands clenched, almost involuntarily. Or you were scared, and your ears seemed dialed into every tiny sound. Or you felt happy, and suddenly the day seemed brighter, smells seemed crisper. Our bodies follow their own kind of truth: the way we physically interact with the world shapes our feelings and vice versa.

Let Your Body Be Your Guide

Musicians learn how to create in rhythm with their bodies, as well as the physicality of their listeners. Why does some music make us want to dance? Because it's in tempo with our flesh and blood. A healthy heart beats around 60 times per minute; an average pop song is around 120 beats per minute. When Lady Gaga's "Bad Romance" or Daft Punk's "Get Lucky" come on the radio, bumping between 116 and 118 bpm, our blood rises, our head starts to bob, and we can't help getting into the groove. Pharrell's "Happy" is 156 bpm; no wonder you can't help dancing to it! But rhythm is just one of many sensations our body can experience from music.

Irish rock band My Bloody Valentine is famous not for creating dance bops but for an indie guitar sound that is enveloping and disorienting, that hits you in the gut, yet is wildly beautiful. Formed in 1983, the band released a series of albums and mini-albums along a journey from rockabilly to punk, but in their live shows, they liked to play loud, raucous sound.

"When we played live, people would double-take, because on the one hand, there were these quiet poppy songs played [in] a garage-band fashion, and we looked kind of funny with the haircuts and stuff, but it was quite painful to listen to," front man Kevin Shields has said. "We used to boost [the frequency] three and a half kilohertz, which is a really horrible frequency to boost. It was all a bit sick, really, and a bit odd."

But it was the release of their album *Loveless* that changed not only the band's lives but also created a new category of rock that the British press snidely called "shoegaze"—which influenced bands like Smashing Pumpkins, Oasis, and Mazzy Star. Like Daniel Johnston and Nirvana, Shields felt that the music of the 1980s was overproduced, using studio effects like reverb to make songs sound pretty.

"I wanted to make everything sound like it was coming out of a ghetto blaster," he said, "just aggressive and the way I actually heard music myself most of the time when I would go to small gigs. [At] small concerts, it's not loads of bass and hi-fi sound. It's mid-range noise with everything fighting to be heard, and it's very exciting sounding and I didn't hear that in music."

He drew particular inspiration from Hank Shocklee's production prowess that created Public Enemy's gritty sound. "They weren't hi-fi hip-hop records," Shields said. "It wasn't music that was designed for an arena, and I loved the up-frontness of that sound and the lack of attempting to pacify the listener with prettiness."

The breakthrough moment for Shields came when a friend lent him a Fender Jazzmaster. The guitar's whammy bar was loose and taped up, allowing him to make the strings shiver in ways he never had been able to achieve before.

"The second I did that, something jumped inside me," he said. "It was the first time in my life I could express an inner feeling in a way that my limited skill level matched to. It allowed me to play in a way where I don't have to think about what I was doing, I just feel it. It was like a stillness or an emptiness, so when I would be recording I wouldn't really see myself as a guitarist playing the music; I would literally be making the sound I was hearing."

The stillness and emptiness that Shields heard in the guitar's sound became the backbone of *Loveless*. In an effort to capture and channel the feeling it gave him—a hypnagogic state of being half asleep, half awake, gliding in and out of the body—Shields decided to use sleep deprivation as a creative strategy. He would not sleep for two to three days at a time, often hallucinating, recording layers and layers of guitars and vocals, mixing them at equal levels so neither came to the forefront, making them seem at once distant and immediate. He faced amplifiers toward one another, causing the sound frequencies to clash and wobble. He used the tremolo bar to bend the notes of full chords, changing their pitch to dizzying effect.

When My Bloody Valentine released the album, Shields expected critics to hate it. But many reviewers were ecstatic. British music magazine *NME* wrote: "*Loveless* fires a silver-coated bullet into the future, daring all comers to try to recreate its mixture of moods, feelings, emotion, styles and, yes, innovations." Ira Robbins wrote in his *Rolling Stone* review: "Despite the record's intense ability to disorient—the effect is strangely uplifting. *Loveless* oozes a sonic balm that first embraces and then softly pulverizes the frantic stress of life." Other critics, of course, disagreed; Martin Aston of British rock rag *Q* said one track from *Loveless* was "especially startling, like a drunken fight between a syrupy Disney soundtrack and an Eastern mantra."

Most students in our class have never heard of My Bloody Valentine—or, frankly, any music like theirs. The shoegaze star burned bright and fast, and within three years was completely eclipsed by Britpop bands Pulp, Blur, and Oasis. When we play the album, we do so without giving any backstory. We simply ask our students to consider how they would describe the music and how it makes them feel. The responses are remarkably consistent, semester after semester. Sometimes a brave student will ask if the speakers are broken or if the producer knew how to use recording equipment! But they almost all use words like: underwater, drifting, woozy, irritated, dreamy, lost, anxious, distant, confused. From drifting to anxious to syrupy, these are perfect adjectives to describe the hypnagogic state. How did they all hear and feel precisely what Shields had attempted to capture and communicate twenty-five years earlier? And what can today's businesses—both brick and mortar and in the digital world—learn from it?

The Science of Sensing

Since we both live in the biotech capital of Boston, we're surrounded by people and companies with a deep curiosity about how music affects the body and mind—and it goes well beyond perception. At Berklee we have the Music and Health Institute, which brings biology and neuroscience to established fields like music therapy. For example, researchers are examining why Alzheimer's patients can recall lyrics of songs from their childhood but struggle to remember their own names. Does music help fire neurons that go otherwise dormant?

They're also exploring questions about music and its curative potential for both mental and physical health. Is music medicine? Can it be prescribed? Might doctors someday recommend a personalized diet of music based on a patient's biometrics? How might virtual immersive experiences aid in unlocking the power of music on the mind?

These fresh new fields of study are building upon decades of academic research exploring how our emotions—activated through our senses of sound, sight, smell, taste, and touch—affect our perceptions and interactions. So how can you benefit from this today? How can being in tune with your body help you distill or articulate an idea? After all, ideas are abstract and intellectual, separate from our bodies—right? Not really, or at least not entirely. Our ideas are intimately connected to our emotions, and an idea is most successful and satisfying (and therefore marketable) when it speaks to our embodied existence.

In today's business climate, rationale and justification are king, particularly when money is on the line. But as you'll remember, Björk and Audur Capital benefited from emotional due diligence—that collaboration is a team built on feeling its way forward. And now that there is wisdom in letting our actual, literal bodies guide our creativity and our communication, it's time to bring in the science.

University of California–Berkeley professor emeritus George Lakoff spent his career researching this idea. He is the coauthor of the 1980 book *Metaphors We Live By*, which explains that the metaphors we use in everyday conversation are actually deep reflections of shared human experience. If I say "that's over my head" about an idea, I'm suggesting the physical experience of being unable to grasp something because it is beyond my reach. Even our use of the word *grasp* is a metaphor: to catch and hold on to an idea.

In the years after publishing his book, Lakoff worked with Vittorio Gallese, professor of psychobiology at the University of Parma, Italy, to back up his theory by using brain scans to trace the paths of active neurons when we encounter metaphors. In a 2005 paper, the two professors wrote that based on multiple studies over the years "meaning in natural language activates imaginative circuitry, that is the same for perception and action." Our minds map pathways between ideas and physicality, so when we are perceiving or imagining, the brain sees it all as action. This gives us clues as to why Yoko Sen was so miserable and unnerved in her hospital room and how Kevin Shields was able to transmit his woozy feelings to others through sound.

Other, more recent studies have built upon Lakoff's research. In a study conducted at Yale, two groups of participants were separated, shown a photograph of a stranger, and asked to evaluate him. Everything that the two groups experienced was the same, except one was given something cold to drink, the other warm. Overwhelmingly, subjects in the study holding the warm beverages evaluated the person in the photo to be generous, while the group holding cold drinks said the stranger was, well, colder. The feeling of warmth, all on its own, stirs feelings of generosity and kindness that we project onto our situation. In another study, researchers from Hong Kong and Colorado studied movie-viewing habits during the coldest months of the year. They found that people tended to watch more heart-warming movies, especially romantic comedies, during winter than in the summer. Not only does warmth produce a feeling of generosity, they deduced, but watching stories about love, kindness, and romance can simulate feelings of physical warmth.

Why do we associate warmth with kindness? Is it because we're held as children? Do our brains draw on memories of floating in water, napping in sunshine, waking from a dream, all of which can be triggered by the sounds or sights that mimic similar feelings? It's hard to say why. What we do know is that warmth is universally soothing, what Lakoff called a metaphor we can live by.

Several years ago, IDEO ran into a challenge with a client who was producing a durable but unattractive spring mattress. Their company's brand prioritized advanced health and technology, and the product needed to communicate this at a glance, but their manufacturing process created a saggy, wrinkled object. In truth, the aesthetics didn't match the reality: it was much more comfortable than it looked. To our designers this was an immediate problem, but the company wasn't convinced that the look was as important as the experience of the product and so worth reinvesting in the manufacturing process. It seemed like a superficial request from beauty-obsessed designers. "People cover their mattresses with sheets so why does this matter?" we were asked.

Gen Suzuki, an IDEO industrial designer, had an idea for persuading the executives to make the investment, which he presented to IDEO management first. He chose two photos of apples and put them on a presentation slide. On the left was a plump, bright red, unblemished apple; on the right was an apple of the same size that was slightly wrinkled from dehydration, partially blemished, and a little less bright. He asked the IDEO team which one we would rather eat. We joked that our parents might have made us eat the old one first before it went bad! But we understood Gen's point immediately: we wanted the fresh apple.

When we showed the slide to the mattress executives in their boardroom, they saw it too. When we followed it up with a slide visually comparing their current ruffled design with our new proposed pillowy design, the decision was made before anyone said a word. The power of the visual couldn't be ignored, no matter how unimportant appearance seemed in abstract conversations two weeks earlier. Creating an image that contained those embodied metaphors that compel us to seek freshness helped these managers get it, and it would help customers get the product's value, too.

Good Luck Chucks

The look and feel of a product, its entire aesthetic profile, has an immense impact on a person's response to it. Why? Because a deeper awareness of your body's reactions to how a thing or idea makes you feel gives you a more immediate and true relationship to it.

Is this ability to tap into sensations just the realm of musicians and designers? Can this sensitivity be learned? Absolutely. In fact, most of us have actually unlearned it—teaching ourselves to resist our feelings and to privilege mind over matter, especially in a business context. But it is a false choice: to think or to feel, to prove or to intuit. With patience and practice, we can develop a sense of entrepreneurial instincts that enable us to feel, as well as think, successfully. Take a moment to go back to our description of the Tourists hotel from Chapter 3: the smell of coffee, the smooth wood walls, the playlist. Did those features make you feel a sense of welcome, of hospitality?

Or think about your favorite pair of Converse Chuck Taylor All Star shoes. Even if you've never owned a pair, chances are good that you have strong, intuitive associations with the brand, perhaps from a clay basketball court as a kid or of the Ramones or the Strokes. Maybe the American hip-hop group N.W.A. who wore Chucks in the biographical film *Straight Outta Compton*, Marty McFly in *Back to the Future*, or even Harry Potter in the movie series' fifth installment, a wardrobe choice that shows he is firmly in his teenage years. The shoes iconically convey attitude, creativity, rebellion. As a general rule, we like to keep our shoes clean—but Chucks are in a different category. They're better when they're scuffed and torn, when they've been scrawled all over with a Sharpie marker. They become a sort of diary.

When Converse came to IDEO to help launch their flagship store, we wanted the store's aesthetic to reawaken these feelings for customers, without spoon-feeding emotions to shoppers through overbranded, hypercurated experiences. So we designed around the idea of "wearing in, not wearing out," applying the vibe to concrete floors that revealed rather than concealed imperfections, reclaimed wooden school gymnasium bleachers with scuffs and carved graffiti, worn leather seating, and hand-drawn signage. When the store opened, it didn't look old or ratty; instead, it was aged with character.

There's a cool parallel in music called decay, where a sound repeats and trails off, almost as if in an echo. The Edge, guitarist for

U2, most famously uses this technique throughout the album *The Unforgettable Fire*. You can also hear it clearly on the opening riff of Guns N' Roses' song "Welcome to the Jungle." Part of its appeal is the aural texture it creates, a literal erosion of sound.

The character of a space shapes our response to it, just as a guitar sound or a fresh apple recalls feelings that live in our bodies. By becoming attuned to these patterns in yourself, and others, you make a very rational choice to let rationality take a back seat.

Letting Go, by Letting Go of a False Choice

Reestablishing the connections between feeling and thinking, between our minds and our bodies, is sometimes associated with the idea of surrender. Surrendering isn't a habit we often ascribe to entrepreneurs: it sounds like defeat. We are not talking about giving up the pursuit of excellence or a dogged persistence in developing a prototype into a fully fledged, go-to-market ready product. By surrender, we mean being open to the unknown and unexpected results that we might uncover.

Brian Eno is a founding member of the 1970s art rock band Roxy Music. He has produced albums for David Bowie, U2, Talking Heads, and Coldplay, among countless others. He is widely credited with inventing ambient music with his record *Discreet Music*, has pioneered generative sound software, composed the famous Microsoft Windows start-up sound, worked as an artist and activist, and can rightly be called rock music's most public intellectual.

In 1975, he was working with painter Peter Schmidt, trading ideas about how they stay creatively sharp. They discovered that they both had a habit of writing down prompts for when they felt stuck and combined their ideas into a deck of unblocking activities. Called *Oblique Strategies*, the prompts take the form of a deck of 3- by 3.5-inch cards.

In an introduction to the cards' 2001 version, Eno and Schmidt wrote: "These cards evolved from separate observations of the principles underlying what we were doing. Sometimes they were recognised in retrospect (intellect catching up with intuition), sometimes they were identified as they were happening, sometimes they were formulated. They can be used as a pack, or by drawing a single card from the shuffled pack when a dilemma occurs in a working situation. In this case the card is trusted even if its appropriateness is quite unclear."

Examples of the cards include:

USE AN OLD IDEA.
WHAT TO INCREASE? WHAT TO REDUCE?
TRY FAKING IT!
DO NOTHING FOR AS LONG AS POSSIBLE.

But among the many aphorisms or suggestions are a surprising number of physical recommendations:

PUT IN EARPLUGS.
MUTE AND CONTINUE.
LOOK AT A VERY SMALL OBJECT. LOOK AT ITS CENTER.
BREATHE MORE DEEPLY.
TAPE YOUR MOUTH.
ASK YOUR BODY.

Oblique Strategies sits in a long tradition of lateral thinking techniques, looking at a problem from a different angle to find new and more appropriate solutions. Their insistence that bodily prompts for imagination help you go beyond the obvious is brilliant and perhaps best encapsulated in the card that simply reads:
GARDENING, NOT ARCHITECTURE.
Eno unpacks this prompt: "We're used to the idea," he said, "that the great triumph of humans is their ability to control. What we're not so used to is the idea that another great gift we have is the talent to surrender. . . . To be able to surrender is to be able

to know when to stop trying to control. And to know when to go with things, to be taken along by them. Our hubris about our success in terms of being controllers has made us overlook that side of our abilities . . . we're so used to dignifying controllers that we forget to dignify surrenderers."

In talking about his own creative journey, Eno described needing to move past the idea that composing is like architecture: "I think like many people, I had assumed that music was produced, or created in the way that you imagine symphony composers make music, which is by having a complete idea in their head in every detail and then somehow writing out ways by which other people could reproduce that. In the same way as one imagines an architect working. You know, designing the building, in all its details, and then having that constructed."

Gardening, he believes, is a more apt metaphor for creativity: "One is carefully constructing seeds, or finding seeds, carefully planting them and then letting them have their life. What this means, really, is a rethinking of one's own position as a creator. You stop thinking of yourself as me, the controller, you the audience, and you start thinking of all of us as the audience, all of us as people enjoying the garden together. Gardener included."

This calls to mind what Yoko Sen told us about her work at Sen Sound: "I think the joy in my work was removing me out of the picture. It's about other people, and it's OK that I don't yet know what the answer will be. My role is to bridge the divide so people get to have a voice. I'm OK with the fact that I don't claim the authorship of that change, that somebody else gets to do it; I got to play a part in creating the ecosystem."

Imagine our delight, after hearing Yoko say these words about addressing the cacophony of medical device bleeps, when we came across a like-minded entry in Brian Eno's diaries from 1995: "July 18: A proposal that car-horns be tunable by their owners. Interesting to see what social harmony or discord would then develop. Also that there should be a car-horn that says 'Thank you' or 'You first' or 'I'm sorry.' Surely if horns were tunable—more like an extension of the voice, then a basic language could quickly develop." Like Björk noticing ships in the harbor in Chapter 1, both Eno and Yoko sensed opportunity in their environments and let their minds wander toward new possibilities.

When we think about the history of business or the evolution of technology, we tend to cast it as a story of human versus nature, carving success out of the rock or the waves through our skill and mastery. But Eno points out that for most of human history, life was unpredictable, subject to plagues, natural disasters, and animal attacks. We like to think of ourselves and our society as more evolved than our ancestors, but we have lost much of their ability to go with the flow, to "navigate and position yourself within the flux of circumstances," as Eno said.

The key, he says, lies in reminding ourselves that we have both a talent for control and a talent for surrender and that both must be kept in balance. "That's what surfers do—take control of the situation, then be carried, then take control," he said. "I want to rethink surrender as an active verb. It's not just you being escapist, it's an active choice. . . . I set up situations that involve abandoning control and finding out what happens."

For Eno, there's both freedom and deeper engagement in trusting not only his own talent but also unknown, unforeseen factors.

"Ecstasy for me can be the feeling of being happy not being in control: trusting that if you let go of the precipice, you're going to be all right," he said. "You don't have to keep fighting the universe; you can stop and the universe is quite good to you."

Interlude 8

We kept this playlist tight, focusing on Yoko K., Kevin Shields, and Brian Eno. All three are shining examples of a musician's ability to tap deep emotions through sound. Keep listening: there's nothing wrong with your headphones.

FIRST CONTACT, Yoko K.
LOOMER, My Bloody Valentine
SOMETIMES, My Bloody Valentine
2HB, Roxy Music
BUBBLE NEST, Yoko K.
SIGNALS, Brian Eno
BAD, U2
PHO, Yoko K.
ONLY ONCE AWAY MY SON, Brian Eno and Kevin Shields

Deep Listening: Low's *Double Negative*, which producer BJ Burton had to master himself because engineers were so confused by the static and distortion in the mix. The first track, "Quorum," creates a sensation of falling, and then the rest of the album feels like you're digging out of the hole.

nine
reinventing

I, Pluralist

In a way you are born again when you go through an experience like this, because life becomes very fresh again.

—Gloria Estefan

A year after David Bowie died, a children's book called *Stardust and Snow* was published by Obverse Books in the UK. In it, author Paul Magrs tells the quite possibly true story of an autistic boy who traveled with his mother to London for a screening of the musical fantasy film *Labyrinth*, which starred Bowie as the Goblin King. The streets of the capital city were crowded with holiday shoppers, picturesque with snow. As the boy made his way into the old Victorian school building where the film was to be shown, he found himself surrounded by the Jim Henson puppeteers with their wild goblins, talking worms, and giant beasts. The scene was loud, bustling, festive—and all a bit much for the boy. He was so withdrawn that Bowie took him aside, removed an invisible mask from his face, and gave it to him.

"Put it on," he said. "It's magic. I always feel afraid, just the same as you. But I wear this mask every single day. It doesn't take the fear away, but it makes it feel a bit better. I feel brave enough then to face the whole world and all the people. And now you will, too."

With that, Bowie created another invisible mask out of thin air and set it on his own face.

"Now we've both got invisible masks. We can both see through them perfectly well, and no one would even know we're wearing them."

Over the course of fifty-four years, Bowie donned one mask after another for his performances: Aladdin Sane, Davy Jones, Halloween Jack, Major Tom, Thin White Duke, Ziggy Stardust, and many others. Looking back over his career, it almost seems that this was his plan all along. In 1971 he released "Changes," the first single from his album *Hunky Dory*. Legend has it that "Changes" was a throwaway song, a parody of nightclub tunes, or even a criticism of musicians chasing fads. But even if it was never meant to define his career, its lyrics were at least prophetic.

With each new stage persona spanning his twenty-six studio albums, Bowie changed his story, his product, even his audience. He synthesized theater, literature, music, film, and even finance (look up Bowie Bonds!), remixing pop culture and delivering it back to us on a silver spoon. Was he confused about his identity? Opportunistically looking for new audiences? We believe that he was showing deep self-knowledge, that he knew who he was, was aware of his strengths and limitations, was confident in his artistic vision, and pursued them with commitment. He knew his truth, and it resonated with others.

When Bowie was inducted into the Rock and Roll Hall of Fame, Madonna presented the award, reminiscing how she snuck out of her father's house to see Bowie in concert.

"I don't think I breathed for two hours. It was the most amazing show that I'd ever seen, not just because the music is great but because it was great theater," she said from the podium. "So unconventional, defying logic and basically blowing my mind. Anyway, I came home a changed woman, as you can see, and my father was not sleeping and he knew exactly where I went, and he grounded me for the rest of the summer. But it was worth every minute that I sat and suffered in my house that summer."

In the years since, Madonna has become known for the chameleon-like reinventions of her career, highlighting one aspect of her personality after another—disco diva, bubblegum pop punk, mistress for the masses, kabbalah guru—challenging norms about sexuality, gender, and, in more recent years, age. With 2019's album *Madame X*, at the age of sixty, she led an all-theater tour of North America and Europe and debuted at the top of the Billboard 200 chart.

On the day he died, she posted on her Facebook wall: "David Bowie changed the course of my life forever. I saw how he created a persona and used different art forms within the arena of rock and roll to create entertainment. I found him so inspiring and innovative. Unique and provocative. A real Genius."

Stefani Germanotta, also known as Lady Gaga, has been a student of Bowie since she was a teenager. In her first music video, she paid homage to her muse by painting the famous Aladdin Sane lightning bolt across her face. And ever since, mimicking the master, she has created spectacle after spectacle, persona after persona. She emerged from a giant plastic egg at the Grammys after seventy-two hours of incubation to sing "Born This Way"; she wore a dress made of raw flank steak to the MTV Music Awards; she sang with a so-called vomit artist at SXSW. But she's also done straightforward performances, the sort expected of a Grammy and Oscar winner, like singing the national anthem at the Super Bowl in a conservative pantsuit. She knows her stage, knows how to read an audience, and makes each opportunity an artistic statement tailored to the situation.

Following a live tribute performance to Bowie, Gaga told Michel Martin of National Public Radio that without Bowie, her life would not have been the same.

"The moment that I saw the Aladdin Sane cover for the first time, I was nineteen years old. It changed my perspective on everything," she said. "I played that record and 'Watch That Man' came on, and that was the beginning of my artistic birth. I had never heard someone with such a strong musical perspective that combined so many genres and types of music in such a boundless way."

"I started to dress more expressively," she said. "I started to be more free with my choices. I started to have more fun. I guess what I'm trying to tell you is, my friends and I, we've lived a lifestyle of total immersion in music, fashion, art, and technology since we were kids. This is because of him. I simply wouldn't be here or have the philosophies that I have if I didn't have someone to look up to that blew my mind so intensely. You know, you meet or see a musician that has something that is of another planet, of another time. It changes you forever."

Bowie, Madonna, and Gaga. Icons like these set an unattainable bar—but only if you view them through the lens of celebrity. Throughout this chapter, we're going to share stories of worldwide megastars and global corporations whose self-knowledge enables remarkable reinvention, but also of how these qualities can shine as brightly in the lives of people who are more like the rest of us.

Coming Back to Earth

Will Dailey calls himself a "middle-class musician." An independent recording artist today, he's a music industry veteran with albums on Universal and CBS. His authentic DIY approach to songwriting has earned music awards, inclusion on the soundtracks of more than fifty television programs and films, and praise from A-listers like Eddie Vedder of Pearl Jam, who said: "His songwriting is just incredible, and it's had a real impact on me." Will is, without question, an accomplished, respected, and successful musician, making it work on his own terms.

We sat down with Will last year to ask his thoughts on reinvention. When we mentioned Bowie, he brightened.

"I remember very young discovering Bowie and realizing that is a god and I am a disciple," he said. "Not like I wanted to sound like him, but I wanted to behave like him."

For Will, part of what made Bowie so inspiring was that the singer lived outside what Will calls "the box": a contrived identity that pigeonholes you into a single genre.

"I'm not saying that's a bad way to go, but if you want to keep the improv muscle completely flat, loose, and open and energized, you have to abandon having a single aesthetic. Like Bowie did. He had a mutating aesthetic. If he came out in khakis and a tie like he was going to open an office, we would have thought it was the coolest. He could have done anything because he never adhered to one thing."

Will has held this value near and dear as he has made his own career choices.

"I feel that when someone says 'oh you sound like this or that,' I get anxious and I go and make something different. It takes a lot of reorganization; you have to keep breaking your own rules but also your own fears, your own doubts, your own pitfalls. The goal, ultimately, is to have a catalogue of songs where any human being could find a song in it that they feel belongs to them, one song that made you feel like you needed it, in this lifetime."

Bowie would have approved. In a series of interviews with CBS's *60 Minutes*, which never aired but were posted on the show's website after he died, he talked about the personal connections that fans forged with his characters.

"In a way I'm very happy I didn't follow through with the idea of trying to convert [Ziggy Stardust] into another presentation. There was an idea of doing a film, but somebody pushed me away saying, 'Why do you want to do that? Why do you want to tie up the loose ends? People have such personalized ideas of who Ziggy Stardust was, you would disappoint a lot of people if you came up with a definitive backstory.' I thought, 'Oh you're right.'"

"Taking away the theatrics and the costuming and the outer layer, I'm a writer," Bowie said. "I started examining the subject matter I write about, and it really only boils down to a few songs based around loneliness to an extent, coupled with isolation, some kind of spiritual search, and a looking for a way into communicating with other people. And that's about it. That's all I've written about for forty years. It hasn't really changed. I've dressed it in different ways throughout my life. Trying to find a different approach each time, trying to find another way into the questions by kind of disarming them, creeping up on them as somebody else."

Reinventing as Business Strategy

Patrick Leddin is an associate professor of managerial studies at Vanderbilt University who has written about Bowie, in particular the correlation between his fluidity and his success. In an article titled "What David Bowie's Career Teaches Us About Strategy," Leddin leans heavily on the work of economist and Harvard Business School professor Michael Porter.

Porter acknowledged that a good test of strategy is a unique value proposition, an idea that is familiar to entrepreneurs and executives alike, but said that it doesn't end there. A great strategy includes "the unique value proposition versus competitors and also a distinctive value chain, involving clear choices about how the company will operate differently to value in line with the value proposition." Since there is no one right way to set yourself apart, "a company's focus should be to choose its customers, understand the customer's needs and compete to be unique, versus competing to be the best."

In music, artists often talk about the importance of finding their own unique, personal voice. Bowie built personas that crossed boundaries, standing out from the other artists of his time—but he did this by creating multiple voices that changed over time.

Porter wrote that while change creates opportunity, it also has potential to create confusion. And in this rapidly evolving world, strategy has to take this into account. Maybe in the past companies set a direction and lived with it for decades. But today that isn't possible. Not only does the strategy for uniqueness need to be set, so does a strategy for constant improvement or what we might call adaptation. It can be challenging to hold both priorities in balance—or, more accurately, in tension—knowing when to prioritize one over the other. But Porter insisted that the two were not mutually exclusive.

"Continuity of strategic direction and continuous improvement in how you do things are absolutely consistent with each other," he wrote. "In fact, they're mutually reinforcing. The ability to change constantly and effectively is made easier by high-level continuity. If you've spent ten years being the best at something, you're better able to assimilate new technologies. The more explicit you are about setting strategy, about wrestling with trade-offs, the better you can identify new opportunities that support your value proposition."

Bowie's guitarist Carlos Alomar said of working with Bowie: "Every time I came back to David, I needed to change. He wanted R&B, rock and roll, electronic music, Emerson, Lake & Palmer, romantic music. Stir the pot and out comes the Thin White Duke. He was such a restless person. He didn't like being comfortable. Comfortable is genre-driven, and be careful, because it will outlive you and it will surpass you. David had a lovely saying, 'Let go, or be dragged.'"

"It was change, change, change," Alomar said. "David would introduce something and leave it."

When Bowie changed his persona and his style, he lost some fans. But he didn't mind; he always moved forward, attracting new audiences as he retained a loyal core following. We believe, like Leddin and Porter, that for companies to succeed decade after decade, attracting new customers, they must understand their core capabilities, strengths, and purpose in ways that allow them to embrace change.

Finding Their Core

Companies have to reinvent to survive in the digital era. Just look at the evolution of Netflix, Slack, or Twitter. But there are examples of long-standing companies that have embraced this path to change. Even if you read about them before, they are worth briefly noting again because of the pattern that emerges through their histories.

Nintendo was founded in Kyoto, Japan, in 1889 as a playing card company. By the 1950s, it had expanded to the United States, growing the business by publishing books on card games. As the company grew rapidly, it expanded into vacuums, hotels, taxis, even noodles, trying to find its next big market. But as those pursuits arrived at dead ends, the company decided to double down on its initial pivot from playing cards to toys.

Nintendo's first big hit was the Ultra Hand, invented by Gunpei Yokoi, a playful engineer working on the manufacturing line who wanted an extending arm for grabbing things in the factory. Later, Yokoi designed electronic toys, accessories for early video games, and eventually the Game Boy. Even though they understood printing, manufacturing, distribution, and global trade, Nintendo's real strength was play.

Nokia, who dominated the mobile category before smartphones, started in 1865 as a wood pulp mill. Over the next hundred years, it grew into a conglomerate that included forestry, cables, rubber boots, tires, and electronics; by the 1980s it had developed the first digital phone as well as the first car phone.

After nearly shuttering in 2013, Nokia sold their phone business to Microsoft and became a 5G network provider. What is the thread of connection here? Nokia's core asset was in creating the ingredients for communication—paper pulp in the early twentieth century, digital networks by the late twentieth. Consider that. From wood pulp, to forestry, to boots and tires, to phone cable, to wireless communication and handsets. That's a journey comparable to Bowie's.

Fujifilm could have faded into obscurity like Kodak did when the digital revolution hit, but it recognized the need to embrace technological change. The company's choices were not as seemingly random as Nintendo's noodles; Fujifilm's core identity was in image reproduction. In 2000, it spent $1.6 billion for a 25 percent stake in cash-strapped Xerox. With the investment, Fujifilm controlled the strategy for the joint venture, FujiXerox, and when the film industry started to founder, it had a cushion of earnings.

In 2007, the same year the iPhone was launched, Fujifilm launched a new venture that leveraged chemistry originally developed for UV protection, which kept color from losing quality in direct sunlight. Reevaluating its identity, Fujifilm realized that its true voice went deeper than reproducing images: it was about keeping images from fading away. So the company founded Astalift, a brand of skin-care products and cosmetics that protects skin from aging due to sun exposure.

And of course, there are many more examples. Look at how National Geographic became a multimedia company, or how IBM pivoted from supercomputers to consulting. It's powerful to see long-established, asset-heavy companies reinventing over and over again. While we're used to this in the software-rich digital age, it's so much more challenging if you own real estate, factories, and inventory. It can be emotionally difficult to make big changes in different ways from those that large digital companies face. In fact, over the years, we've seen a lot of companies like this lose the nerve required to make changes, but this nerve is also needed for them to survive. And understanding their core strengths is the only way they have been able to succeed.

Making It Personal

You might be thinking: good stories, but I'm not a one-hundred-year-old corporation. How are these stories relevant to my own personal and professional journey? In the years since we started sharing the ideas in this book with entrepreneurs, musicians, and students, we have met many people who took the time to understand themselves and leveraged what they learned to navigate their careers.

Jen Trynin is one such musician who single-handedly reinvented her sound into a major record contract and then reinvented herself again when it all came crashing down. In 1995, the *Los Angeles Times* wrote: "Imagine a cross between soft-shelled Marti Jones and hard-case Liz Phair and you're getting fairly close to Jen Trynin, who with this preternaturally accomplished debut . . . has made an unassumingly great little rock 'n' roll album." *Spin* magazine wrote that her song "One Year Down" "perfectly captures the inability to heal a broken heart, and does so catchily and without resorting to clichés or sappiness."

We met with her one autumn afternoon in 2019. She had the same mussed hair and the same motorcycle boots she'd worn when we met her at an art exhibit eighteen months earlier. Since that time, her husband, producer Mike Deneen, had passed away, and she had started writing a book about loss—reflecting on Mike's cancer and trying to make sense of life—a presumed follow-up to her 2006 autobiography *Everything I'm Cracked Up to Be: A Rock & Roll Fairy Tale*.

We asked Jen about her own journey from rock star to author and back again. With incredible vulnerability and self-awareness, she took us back to the early days of her career when she was struggling to break into Boston's music scene as a folk acoustic artist.

"I did OK for a while when I was in college. I played out in the summers at resort places and restaurants," she said. "It seemed like it was working. When I moved to Boston, I was like, 'I'm going to play in some jazz clubs.' But then I was just getting blocked out."

So in 1994. she walked away from the folk-jazz scene, strapped on an electric guitar, toughened her sound, and independently released an album called *Cockamamie.* Suddenly, she was the hottest commodity in rock music.

"I changed my wrapping, and it literally happened in a matter of weeks. I didn't change the songs, really, I just changed the way I presented them. That really is all it was. It's different from changing what you're doing creatively. To me there's the art, and then there's the wrapping."

Jen wasn't prepared for what happened next: a flood of promises and propositions from major record labels. In *Everything I'm Cracked Up to Be,* she writes: "The lights are low, everything swirling with drinks and hands and teeth, and the talk is fast: priority, roll out, capitalize, maximize, merchandise, marketing." In the mid-1990s, before the digital revolution put more control in the hands of artists, the labels reveled in big egos, sleazy glory, and hyperdictating the images of their artists. At first, Jen capitulated, foregoing her own identity for a shot at the big stage; she became what she was asked to be, a supercool alt-rock phenomenon who wore silly clothes and acted obnoxious.

But eventually she pushed back. "That's what is most fascinating to me looking in the rearview," she told us. "Am I going to wear one of those too-big, boxy shirts with stripes on it from the GAP because that's what all the other old rock people are wearing? No."

As she asserted herself, the labels pulled back, and the promises of stardom faded. As the label turned its focus to Alanis Morissette, the former child actress turned gritty diva, Jen found herself sent out on the road to play gigs in small clubs. Eventually, she stepped away from that life to focus on writing and in 2015 formed a new band called Cujo, on her own terms. She explained that the band, much like her previous and current books, is a kind of creative catharsis, a way of understanding and coping with life's mysteries, the good and the bad.

"In Cujo, I'm some hard-ass rock chick," she said. "That's the persona. I'd never done that before, and it's so fun—the older I get, the more fun it is. I know I'm too old to do this, but I genuinely don't care when I'm up there playing."

Dr. Kristen Ellard is a clinical fellow in psychology at Massachusetts General Hospital. But in the 1990s, she was Kristen Barry, a rising star in Seattle's grunge scene, being groomed to become "the female Soundgarden." At the time, she shared living and practice digs with Alice in Chains; played with Heart, Matchbox Twenty, and the Sneaker Pimps; and released her own album on the Virgin label. But then the new head of Virgin dropped her; the rumor was that someone left her photo on his desk with the words "big mistake" written across it in a black marker. By then, she had started hearing about Morissette, whom the label had chosen to back. Apparently, alternative rock radio only had room for one female artist at a time.

Three years later, Warner Brothers called and said that they were blown away by her work, wanted to resurrect her career, and recommended that she collaborate with the cowriter of the theme song from NBC's sitcom *Friends*. But in a bold move, she hung up. Kristen knew who she was, the driving force behind her music, and wanted to build upon it in new directions. A decade later, she completed her PhD in psychology.

"My whole life I had been curious about people," she told us. "So when I found science, things opened back up for me. Suddenly, I was back in a place where I was thinking about human experience and human existence, which is not that different from what I was doing with my music."

She shared an analogy from her research in psychiatric neuroscience: "It's amazing how many people in psychiatric research are just looking for symptom reduction without thinking about how they're affecting behavior, how they're going up against evolutionary forces. I want it to be more meaningful than just finding a significant P value and writing a paper. How can we use what we have learned to improve upon what we have? I'm always the annoying person in the room saying 'Yeah, but what does this mean?' I think I'm able to do that because of the way I have approached music. I was always on the outside, I've never played by the rules, and that gives me an incredible freedom to constantly be questioning."

André Obin works in the Department of Materials Science and Engineering at MIT. He also is a working electronic musician with an enviable pedigree that includes US and European tours, technopop singles, and several album releases. Weaving genres of techno and shoegaze, he's collaborated with indie icons like Mark Gardener from Ride and remixed songs for rising stars including Avoxblue, CMB, Kodacrome, the Foreign Resort, and People at Parties.

André told us that his skills in music recording and production are expressed daily at MIT. While he's not a scientist, he understands storytelling and collaborates with the researchers to help them communicate ideas. His role is synthesis in action, taking significant amounts of information, finding connections, and communicating them simply.

"I feel like a concierge for scientists," he said. "As an artist and a musician, I have a good insight into what their desires are as engineers. There are millions of simple ideas that they're trying to build into something, sometimes future oriented, sometimes it's trying to solve gigantic problems with small things."

André is able to feed both music and his day job simultaneously, learning from one and applying it to the other.

"I was told growing up that science is a separate path from music," he said. "At this point in 2019, it seems almost crazy to think that. I see, in real time, how the lines are blurring because of technology and the way our minds are changing. As we move forward, the lines between science, art, design, engineering will be blurred to a point where rock stars will be neuroscientists all the time."

Reinventing out of Necessity

In some of these situations, both corporate and artistic, the re-inventors explored new paths out of a desire to express their true voice. In others, the choice was forced upon them. They were dropped by a label, or their core industry started to falter. This kind of reinvention takes on the urgency of necessity. It still involves choice but also a lot of uncertainty.

As we were writing this chapter in March 2020, the COVID-19 pandemic hit. Early in the month, it was business as usual in the United States with some foreboding headlines coming from overseas. A couple of weeks later, our cities were ghost towns. Nations militarized their borders, and the global stock markets tanked. "Work from home" was no longer a perk; it became a mandate. At Berklee, we closed our campuses in Boston, New York, Valencia, Spain, and Abu Dhabi and sent 6,500 students home; professors scrambled to shift their entire perspective on and methodology of academic instruction from on-campus to virtual. At IDEO, we were challenged to rethink core practices like human-centered field research, collaboration, and prototyping—as well as to help our clients make deep shifts in their own systems, work cultures, and sense of self.

Out in the broader marketplace, product designers and manufacturers stepped into the gap, reinventing in the moment. Ford collaborated with General Electric's health-care division to speed up the production of ventilators, desperately needed in hospitals around the world.

Dyson, the manufacturer of high-design, high-performance vacuum cleaners, fans, and hand dryers, designed a completely new ventilator specifically for COVID-19 patients—in just ten days. The ventilators can be mounted to a bed and run on batteries, making them ideal for use in field hospitals that were set up in New York and Barcelona.

Smaller companies responded, too. Disc Makers, a New Jersey manufacturer of CDs, DVDs, USBs, and other media for independent musicians, pivoted to make protective face shields for medical personnel and first responders.

This capability to pivot, even if just temporarily, is inspiring during a time of such bad news. But it's not just companies showing resilience. In the midst of the chaos, we found ourselves also inspired, once again, by musicians. In China, where the pandemic was at its peak in February 2020, nightclubs hosted virtual DJ shows for people stuck at home. When singer and rapper Cardi B posted a rant on Instagram, shouting, "Let me tell y'all something, I ain't even gonna front. A bitch is scared. Coronavirus. Shit is real. Shit is getting real," the Brooklyn DJ iMarkkeyz remixed the audio into a song. Fans looking for a distraction and a bright spot in a bleak month took the track to number four on the iTunes hip-hop chart; both the singer and DJ donated revenues to people affected by the disease.

For decades now, we've watched as other musicians have embraced this kind of reinvention. In high school, we were both fans of Def Leppard and remember being shocked to hear that drummer Rick Allen had lost his left arm in a car accident shortly after the release of *Pyromania*. Yet two years later, he was back behind the kit, touring to promote the group's new album *Hysteria*—which had a very different sound. Def Leppard had moved from a gritty hard rock to a polished pop rock sheen.

In March 1988, Allen said that the hospital staff set a piece of foam rubber at the foot of his bed to keep him from sliding down. As he lay in recovery, he started tapping on it, working out rhythms with his feet.

"I got my brother to bring down my stereo system, and I started playing all my favorite albums again, as I sort of tapped along to them," he said. "There were a few things that were a bit difficult because I had only played a single bass drum, so it took a lot of concentration to get my feet working right."

Less than a month later, he asked a local friend who tinkered with electronics to help build specially designed electronic foot pedals.

"He actually built me a prototype pedal. I started trying it out, and I figured, 'This is going to work. There's no reason why it can't,'" Allen said. "Cosmetically, the look of the kit hasn't really changed all *that* much. But obviously, technology-wise, I'm exploring other paths. I'm getting into different kinds of equipment, but basically, it's down to the sound now. And my playing is getting better month by month the more I do it."

He said his main takeaway from the experience was perseverance. "I guess that would be the biggest thing I learned about myself. But I suppose that had a lot to do with the strength of those around me. They really didn't give me a choice; I had to stick around and deal with it."

In his determination to overcome the obstacle, to improvise and create a new normal, Allen found strength that overcame self-doubt. And along the way, he invented the electronic drum kit. *Hysteria*'s new sound was wildly successful, charting at number one on both the Billboard 200 and the UK Albums Chart. Looking back on the changes, the band's guitarist Phil Collen said: "Rick's kit made the album sound different from anything else out there. It fit perfectly with [our producer]'s aim of creating a new genre . . . bring[ing] pop elements and other things into our sound."

Turn the Beat Around

In 2017, we were invited by Gloria and Emilio Estefan to attend a showing of *On Your Feet!*, the Tony Award–nominated Broadway musical about their lives and careers. We're old friends from the music industry, so we met in the lobby before the show. It was funny seeing theatergoers walk past the power couple without noticing, not expecting them to be there. In their typical way, they did nothing to call attention to themselves. They live a private life, centered on family, but aren't shy about stepping into the spotlight when it can help others.

Through act one, we watched flashbacks from their life, from Gloria as a child sending recordings of her songs to her father stationed in Vietnam, through her hesitancy giving up her psychology studies to perform, to her budding relationship with Emilio.

Act two opens with the pair at the top of the US Adult Contemporary charts, exhausted from touring, but pushing across the country to play a show in Syracuse. Then, the bus accident.

En route to New York, the band's tour bus was stopped on a snowy highway in traffic, after a truck had jackknifed up ahead, when a tractor-trailer truck smashed into them. Gloria was sleeping in a bunk and was thrown to the floor, breaking her spine and knocking the bones out of alignment. Her nine-year-old son's collar bone was broken, and Emilio was knocked unconscious. In the hospital, two titanium rods were inserted to brace her spine, and doctors told her that she might never walk again and would likely not be able to perform.

Recovery took her more than a year.

"It was the first time in my life that I had nothing I could possibly do or nowhere I could possibly go," she said. "I really didn't know how to get back into the writing routine because I was feeling so alien to being normal. My confidence was shaken."

But Emilio encouraged her to get up, not to give up, to persist with therapy.

"He told me about an idea that came to him as I was being transported from one hospital to the next," she said. "He saw the sun coming up from behind the clouds and wished so much that time would pass and this would all be behind us, so he came up with a line: 'Coming out of the dark.'"

In a quiet but powerful conversation at Berklee, Gloria told us about her days fighting to walk again.

"The only way to reach the long-term goal is to focus every day on what you can do that day. It was much easier for me to be lying down; there was a lot of pain involved. I had to talk myself into getting out of bed: 'Today I'm going to walk to the doorway. Tomorrow I'm going to take a few more steps to the hall. The following day I'm going to try to do a little more than that.' It didn't matter if that day I only went one inch past what I had done the day before, the whole key was to do something more because I knew that if I did nothing, I would take three steps back."

"You can take that analogy and put it to anything that's going on in your life," she said. "How am I going to try today to be just a little better than I did yesterday? And then, on those days that you screw up, it becomes about: OK, I'll start again tomorrow."

At this point in the conversation, Gloria paused to look at the students gathered around our conversation and said: "We need people who have initiative and who are proud of the work they do. The world is getting too comfortable; people want to do the least possible for the most amount of money, and that's not going to get you a lot of success. If I can encourage you to do one thing, it's to be the employee you want to have working for you or be the musician you want to be playing with. You've got to sharpen your tools because the more you learn the better you can be."

Bursting at the Seams

Coming full circle, our last chapter is about new beginnings. About knowing yourself and making the decision to explore new possibilities and new expressions, in both dark times and light. Reinvention is always a choice, as are listening, experimenting, collaborating, demoing, connecting, producing, remixing, sensing, and surrender. Each one demands knowing yourself and putting in the effort to understand your unique voice and vision, and each one requires practice. Charlie Parker, the legendary saxophonist who redefined jazz and created bebop through his flaming virtuosity and revolutionary play with harmonics, once said: "You've got to learn your instrument. Then, you practice, practice, practice. And then, when you finally get up there on the bandstand, forget all that and then just wail."

At some point, you have to let go, trusting your own voice and your unique understanding of the world that is always unfolding around us. Throughout these chapters, you've heard stories of both musicians and entrepreneurs who chose not to conform to the shoulds and shouldn'ts, cans and can'ts that others told them. Perhaps you've experienced those moments, too, from record labels or bosses or even prevailing wisdom: What is right or wrong for an artist or businessperson? Who makes these rules? We believe that you can. As Parker also said: "Music is your own experience, your thoughts, your wisdom. They teach you there's a boundary line to music, but man, there's no boundary line to art." And art is everywhere. You can play the chords and riff on them, too. Know your markets and create new ones; find your gifts and connect with other people's. Being open to new possibilities and capable of exploring and adapting to them with a musician's mindset. When you do, you'll find that not only can it open new doors for you, it becomes a way of life.

In our conversation with Pharrell at Berklee's Career Jam, he reminded us that this openness is not only a skill that comes with time and effort, it also becomes a way of life.

"I'm just always curious about new sounds, new textures, new ways of expressing myself. I think curiosity is where it begins for me, and I don't know that it's necessarily a habit so much as a gift and a blessing."

Looking out at the faces of our students, he said: "There are a lot of people who focus on one thing singularly and that works for them. But for a lot of us, a lot of people in this generation and a lot of people in the audience today, we're pluralists. We need multiple outlets. We need to be able to express ourselves in different ways."

Our conversation with Hank Shocklee ended on a similar note:

"The model today is Jay-Z, Beyoncé, Cardi B, Rihanna, Kanye. You can't pin them down; they're multidimensional creatives. Beyoncé is an amazing singer, but that's not all she does. You look at Erykah Badu, she's DJ'ing. Why is Jay-Z such a great businessman? He understands the root, and the root is always going back to the vibrations, and the vibrations are always going to lead back to people."

He paused, as if thinking for a moment about all that he's seen in his career, in studios and boardrooms.

"The amount of creativity that's coming out of every corner today is overwhelming; it's fucking amazing. What happens next isn't going to be determined by the old system; it's going to be determined by us, the creators."

Interlude 9

For our final chapter, we made a playlist from the trinity of change: David Bowie, Lady Gaga, and Madonna. The songs span forty years of pop, show tunes, EDM, and soundtracks that remind us that when we understand our core strengths, our careers and personas can be fluid and faceted.

FAME, David Bowie

LIKE A VIRGIN, Madonna

RAY OF LIGHT, Madonna

I'M AFRAID OF AMERICANS, David Bowie

BAD ROMANCE, Lady Gaga

LUSH LIFE, Lady Gaga and Tony Bennett

THIS IS NOT AMERICA, David Bowie and Pat Metheny Group

CHEEK TO CHEEK, Lady Gaga and Tony Bennett

CHANGES, David Bowie

CHILLY DOWN, David Bowie (*Labyrinth* soundtrack)

HEROES, David Bowie

Deep Listening: Bowie's duets: "Fame" with John Lennon, "Young Americans" with Luther Vandross, "Under Pressure" with Queen, "Dancing in the Street" with Mick Jagger, "Reflektor" with Arcade Fire, and "Fame '90" with Queen Latifah. It's worth googling stories of his work with Lou Reed and Iggy Pop; Bowie was responsible for reenergizing their careers. In each case, it's as if he amplified the eccentricities of each genre and the vision of each artist he touched.

coda

The word *coda* comes from Italian for "tail." In music, it's a passage that brings a piece to an end, although technically it's an expanded cadence, a configuration of notes that creates a sense of resolution or at least of pause. We like that meaning for this final chapter: we started this book as a conversation with each other, with an amazing array of musicians and entrepreneurs and with you as a reader. So it's not really an ending.

On a crisp September evening in 2019, we spent an hour with Roger Brown, Berklee's president, to ask for his perspective on the thesis of this book. Always a teacher, always an entrepreneur, he took what he learned as a high school teacher in Kenya and applied it to the start-up Bright Horizons serving young children and then again in service of students at Berklee College. When Roger took the post of president in 2004, he was only the third president since Berklee was founded in 1945, but he has perhaps been the most entrepreneurial one. Under his leadership, the college expanded significantly, establishing a graduate school in Valencia, Spain; launching supplemental music programs for public schools;

launching Berklee Online and merging with the 150-year-old Boston Conservatory. Roger also helped establish graduates as business leaders in the music industry, most recently Silicon Valley. At every step along the way, he's looked forward into the future. Perhaps this is an inevitable part of being involved in education, but with Roger it's a core principle.

"I think the arc is you can make the world a better place through education," he told us in his easy southern drawl. "I saw the same thing in my refugee relief work, trying to create opportunity for people. Education shows up in a lot of different forms."

"There's a great joke told by a house parent at Harvard who was also teaching at Berklee at the same time: 'When a young person is admitted to Harvard, it's usually because of eighteen years of effort on the part of the entire extended family. When a young person chooses to go to Berklee, it's usually over the objections of the entire extended family,'" he shared with a chuckle. "There's truth in it. Any student who chooses to come here has probably had to argue with someone who said, 'How are you going to make a living? What job are you going to get?'"

But from his first days at Berklee, he noticed a pattern among students that he felt should be amplified:

"I saw that almost all of our students, with exception of those who get hired by a public school to be a teacher or a hospital to be a music therapist, are entrepreneurs—even though they may not have labeled themselves as such. I also saw that compared to many music schools, our students were already behaving entrepreneurially, playing in wedding bands, forming ensembles, getting gigs. Some of them even started businesses while they were here."

In those early years, there was no curriculum to codify, develop, or support these behaviors. And the longer he was in office, the more strongly he believed teaching students to think and act like an entrepreneur was more critical than ever. Things finally clicked when he met Panos. Roger was on the Board of Directors of Panos's company Sonicbids, and after Panos sold the company,

Roger saw an opportunity to hire a Berklee alum with successful entrepreneurial experience. His direction to Panos was reminiscent of Beyoncé's instructions of "do your thing" to her collaborators.

"I had this germ of an idea, and I had this guy who I thought would be pretty amazing doing it, who knew the school and who knew the industry," Roger said. "We coengineered the idea. I didn't have any microplan. I basically said to Panos, 'You'll figure it out.'"

Panos joined Berklee and founded Berklee Institute for Creative Entrepreneurship (BerkleeICE) in 2014. He had just begun figuring out his new life in academics, feeling his way forward, meeting with Silicon Valley venture capitalists as well as students, and soon found himself on the lecture circuit, sharing ideas about musical thinking and entrepreneurship. A few months into his new gig, in June 2014, Panos was scheduled to speak at a conference in Boston on this very topic but woke up that morning second-guessing his participation. He hates morning meetings, likes to wake up early to work out then eat breakfast in silence, and considered skipping the event, including his own presentation! But at the last minute decided to go.

As it turns out, Michael was also slated to speak at that conference and felt that he was at a crossroads in his career. After a long road from freelance designer to founding a hybrid tech-design company to taking on a leadership role at IDEO, he had spent twenty years helping designers and entrepreneurs grow on a daily basis. But he was burned out on the topic and wanted to spend more time on a discipline that is close to his heart: music.

Both of our careers have taught us that at times of transition, when you need new thoughts or to explore new ideas, it's smart to keep your ears open, to listen with intention. It's also often a great time to seek out a collaborator. Michael went to Panos's presentation and felt a real resonance: here was an entrepreneur who works for one of the country's preeminent colleges of music, talking about how creativity and business intersect and overlap.

So Michael chased Panos down the hall and introduced himself. Panos's response was to invite him to teach a class at Berklee. Neither of us had ever met or worked together before, but we felt an intuitive connection of ideas and thought it'd be worth a risk. The risk wasn't haphazard; it was grounded in mutual respect, not worrying about whether one of us was going to upset the other, being willing to deal with any fallout later. We've said it before in these pages: it's like two musicians coming together. Even if they've never played together before, they know how to step forward, step up to the mic, and then also step back and let their collaborators step forward. As we got to know each other better, this mutuality became even more clear. We both were leading our own organizations through a moment of immense, rapid change. Berklee was expanding globally and growing its programs at its home campus in Boston. With ICE, Panos was at the center of the local growth and soon would be at the helm of the global changes, expanding Berklee's presence into New York, China, and the Middle East. Michael was supporting teams as IDEO strengthened its global reach and helping see the company through a period of transition.

But here's the funny part: even though we were executives in respected businesses, we each had a tinge of imposter syndrome. No one taught us how to do this. Plus, we looked like the yin-yang rhythm section of an indie jam band! Panos with his wide mohawk, Michael with his shoulder-length bedhead. The confidence we had came from our previous professional experience as entrepreneurs. Both of us had built our own companies upon similar instincts, which we would eventually codify in this book. We had also noticed that the tools to make music and design were coming together through a figurative software singularity. Software was lowering the barrier to entry into the creative arts, and digital workspaces were beginning to look the same. Constructing a song didn't feel that different from editing a photo. The tools were digitally native, born from the same binary ones and zeros, and expressing themselves with nearly identical user interfaces—and so the kids using them were, too. We put all of these ingredients into our classes with ICE, bridging concepts from design thinking, music creation, and entrepreneurship. We prototyped this lecture for several semesters, eventually hosting the class at IDEO in Cambridge, Massachusetts, instead of the coworking space, and turning it into a semester course. We moved beyond noting entrepreneurial traits to helping the students claim and act upon them. Some of them just wanted to build their own brands as artists; others had ideas for new production gear. Sometimes we dabbled in territory that was a far cry from the music industry. We remember one student who had recently gone through a medical issue that resulted in complex billing and the frustration and confusion that comes with such situations. He wanted to design electronic medical records! Another semester we turned the attention of the class on Berklee itself, having the students redesign the career services for the college. Even though these applications might sound way off base for music college students, we didn't see it as a stretch. The creative mindsets inherent in these students simply needed to be unleashed.

Today, The Creative Entrepreneurial Mindset is the foundational course of the creative entrepreneurship minor at Berklee. As it has grown in popularity, the students have diversified. Our first semester class was made up of performance and production majors in their junior and senior years. Today, thanks to Berklee's merger with the Boston Conservatory, our class includes not only jazz and pop performers and producers but also songwriters, classical musicians, actors in contemporary theater, and classical and modern dancers—from freshmen to seniors. And through an innovative program that encourages students from nearby arts colleges to take classes at sister schools, we even have the pleasure of teaching fine arts majors, screenwriters, and graphic designers.

We also have expanded this application outside the curriculum. In 2016 Berklee and IDEO created a summer start-up lab for the Open Music Initiative, an industry consortium we cofounded with entrepreneur and Berklee trustee Dan Harple to promote open source standards and to help assure proper compensation for music creators.

The eight-week program explored how data might be collected during creative workflow and new experiences could be created for both artists and fans using blockchain. Students from the Rhode Island School of Design, the Maryland Institute College of Art, Harvard, MIT, Tufts, and Berklee created five multidisciplinary teams resulting in twelve new concepts and prototypes. At the end of the summer, on the top floor of the MIT Media Lab, the students shared their work with Open Music Initiative members comprising nearly three hundred companies from the tech and music industries, including Universal Music, Sony Music, YouTube, Spotify, Netflix, Facebook, Intel, IBM, and dozens of blockchain start-ups.

One team created a prototype called On Record, a quarter-inch adapter plug with a unique sonic identifier or sound print assigned to an individual musician and integrated into her recording path. This embedded information is captured during a performance and then permanently embedded into the recorded track, eliminating the need for metadata that identifies the artist. Musicians who contribute to a song can forever be identified by scanning the song file, making it easier to compensate them for their art.

The initiative also opened up new listening opportunities for fans. Another team prototyped a new streaming platform they named INTRSTLR. The concept takes advantage of song contributor information (embedded through a device like On Record) and helps build a following for lesser-known or unknown musicians, producers, and engineers. Since the family tree of contributors on each song is easily identified, listeners can follow these creators, for example a bass player or back-up vocalist, through their entire portfolio of work.

We repeated this lab again in 2017 with a new mix of students and support from the Inter-American Development Bank—with a view to encouraging blockchain use in the Caribbean. Again, the results were exciting, producing new artist and listener experiences. In the two years that have passed since the first program, we have seen a noticeable shift in our student body: they are increasingly more proficient in using technologies to blur the lines among creative disciplines.

Design thinking is grounded in a profession that has making at its core and has in recent years been placed at the center of innovation and, by extension, of economic growth. Its tenure there has created a rich vocabulary and well-documented practices that produce real results. The students certainly used elements of this practice, but they also expanded and redefined it as they transferred their musical minds to new applications.

Teaching students from such a wide variety of backgrounds has confirmed the common ground—even a common mindset—among *all* creative professions. The craftsmanship of its application may differ for graphic artists, pianists, ballet dancers, actors, writers, and others and is mastered through years of practice, but the creative and entrepreneurial roots come from the same place. This is both freeing and energizing. Thinking like a designer or musician or dancer or actor or screenwriter or company founder or fill-in-the-blank starts with shared perspectives.

As our collaboration has grown, like any good band, we've found that we're both creative and business partners. There is a baseline assumption in this relationship that we won't screw each other over from a business standpoint; neither is going to do something unscrupulous. But it goes deeper, into an expectation of reciprocity. Each of us has always expected to learn and to grow with the other. We want to build something together, to make something together, even if there isn't a real strong sense of what the result would be.

All of which led to this book—our first album together, if you will. At the start, it was just us comparing notes, discussing the shared mindsets of designers and musicians, finding places of alignment, and articulating them together. Listening, observing, shared prototyping around an iterative soul. The multidisciplinary approach to problem solving was similar to the dynamics of a band—each of us brought our expertise to create a sum bigger than the individual. Even our ideas about leadership were relevant: seeing it as a fluid role to play versus a set hierarchical model.

The first real test of this collaboration came when, after a year and a half of working on the book, we both felt that it was dead in the water. We believed in our ideas, the interviews we had been lucky enough to conduct were amazing, and the content was really interesting, but we had been working with content developers who just didn't seem to get it. We were both struggling, struggling, struggling; it felt like we were on a seesaw, losing our minds over why the dots didn't seem to connect. As with so many creative projects, we had a time line from our editors; we had each invested a tremendous amount of energy into the project, and the idea of walking away from it was hard. We had to make a change. Even at that critical point in the book, we looked to each other and our shared belief that this could be helpful and impactful. We wanted to take a real stand that creative education is under threat. In an era where we apply efficiency on everything—how we interact with each other, how we solve problems—we have stripped humanity out of so many things. Why have we, as a society, swung the pendulum so far to the analytical side? Why is everybody talking about teaching young girls and young boys to code, but almost no one is talking about the urgent need to really get young people to think creatively, think imaginatively?

In our conversation with T Bone Burnett, he gave some insight: "There were decisions made in the last century; we became more and more organized around systems. Within the school system, for example, there were decisions made about the most efficient way to teach children that stripped art out of the school system because art is the opposite of efficient. Art has nothing to do with efficiency, and efficiency has nothing to do with art. Art is inspired, or it's not art."

"So what is inspiration?" he said. "Inspiration is not efficient. Inspiration is like the wind: it blows, and we can't see it. We can't see the wind, but we can see it blow the trees, right? But it's not efficient. Sometimes it blows the trees down, sometimes it blows a tree onto your house. Yet we have an excessive emphasis of algorithms and digits, and engineering disciplines, and mathematics. In my view, those disciplines are absent of humanity, and creativity is ultimately humanity's most important ability. Creativity is the big bang. It's the genesis. There would be no mathematics if it wasn't for human beings' infinite creativity. There would be no science because creativity's embedded within science and not the other way around. That conversation is absent."

But there certainly is hope. In the past three decades of our own careers, we have often thought about how much power is now in the hands of individuals, and how this sea change happened. In our view, it's because Apple flattened out access to creativity through its intuitive interfaces and disruptive software tools. When Michael graduated from university, he had friends who were typesetters for offset printing presses. Today, anyone with simple tools like iMovie, Photoshop, Garage Band, and SketchUp can create production-quality products. The talent and experience might not always be there, but the possibility is. Apple's "Shot on iPhone" campaign, launched in 2015, proves the point: anyone with an iPhone version 6 or later can shoot photographs at such high quality that they can be printed for a billboard, without being retouched.

When we asked entrepreneur Steve Stoute for his thoughts on this, he said: "How come no one talks about this? There were huge industries that got completely eaten up. What was once professional equipment was suddenly usable for a hobbyist, for the everyday person. Everywhere I look, I see artists working on so many projects that previous generations would not have had the chance or ability to do. If you're truly talented and are willing to lean into opportunities to apply that talent to different form factors, it'll just keep multiplying."

So we retooled, rewrote, reimagined, reinvented. And ultimately, we looked to the many creators you have met throughout the book: an avant-pop electronic musician founding a venture fund, a six string virtuoso designing a new guitar, a pioneer of early electronics founding a cloud storage business, a bassist launching a hotel, a composer developing wearable musical gloves, a drummer founding a microphone cable company, an ambient electronic musician redesigning the sounds of medical equipment, a rock star becoming a neuroscientist—and, of course, an R&B singer launching sneakers, sunglasses, and cologne. Though they come from different backgrounds and even different generations, they share a perspective, a musical mindset, that shapes how they approach the world. Our hope is that we create an ongoing conversation, bringing ideas together from many disciplines.

As Hank Shocklee told us: creative people are not just limiting themselves to just creative areas anymore.

"We're multidimensional beings," he said. "People who step into this, those are the kinds of people that are going to make the future. They're going to replace people who are one dimensional. Those who don't understand are out of step, out of key, out of tune, out of time. A CEO of a company had better be able to go rock some beats at the local club down the street. And if he can't do that, then he's not using his full multidimensional capabilities, and he's going to be beat out by somebody who does."

"We're moving from one age to another," he said. "When you move from one age to another, there's going to be major disruption, just like there was shifting to the Industrial Age from the Agricultural. Now we've moved from the Industrial to the Digital. We're hitting that bump right now that's going to unlock the

energy that's been held back for so long, that's been held back under these old paradigms of what we used to do before. Now the
only way forward for us is through creativity—creativity which we
have an enormous abundance of. The old system has a hard time,
if anything, trying to deal with all that energy that's coming out.
But if you look at the world today, it's bursting at the seams with
creative people. There are millions of them out there, right now.
Millions."

samples (aka bibliography)

In music, sampling is the reuse of bits and pieces of another artist's work. As writers working at the intersection of music and entrepreneurship, we've been lucky to sit down with accomplished musicians and business innovators to talk about the ideas in this book, but we've also drawn on fascinating conversations with other interviewers, other authors. To give credit where credit's due, we've cited them by chapter.

Prelude

Banks, Alice. "Pharrell Williams Describes His Design Style and Working with Adidas." Highsnobiety, May 17, 2016. www.highsnobiety.com/2016/05/17/pharrell-williams-adidas-interview/.

Cheung, Adam. "A Brief History of the Pharrell Williams x Adidas Originals NMD Hu." Sole Supplier, August 29, 2018. https://thesolesupplier.co.uk/news/brief-history-pharrell-williams-x-adidas-originals-nmd-hu/.

Gardner, Chris. "Pharrell Williams on Adidas Collaboration: I'll Never Be a Michael Jordan." *Hollywood Reporter*, December 4, 2014. www.hollywoodreporter.com/news/pharrell-williams-adidas-collaboration-ill-753967.

Hague, Matthew. "Oh, Heyyy, Pharrell." *Matthew Hague* (blog). February 17, 2020. https://matthewhague.com/2020/02/17/oh-heyyy-pharrell/#more-1064.

HB Team. "Pharrell Talks Music, Fashion and Design." Hypebeast, January 3, 2013. https://hypebeast.com/2013/1/pharrell-talks-music-fashion-and-design.

Mitchell, Julian. "Pharrell, Pusha T and Torben Schumacher Discuss How Adidas Became the Global Brand for Creators." *Forbes*, December 18, 2018. www.forbes.com/sites/julianmitchell/2018/12/18/pharrell-pusha-t-and-torben-schumacher-discuss-how-adidas-became-the-global-brand-for-creators/#581b204318a9.

Skelton, Eric, and Pierce Simpson. "Pharrell Williams Talks Kanye West, Kid Cudi, Adidas, and More." Complex, November 15, 2018. www.complex.com/music/2018/11/pharrell-interview-kanye-west-kid-cudi-solar-hu-adidas.

Socha, Miles. "How Pharrell Williams and Adidas Are Trying to Chip Away Racial Barriers." Footwear News, September 26, 2016. https://footwearnews .com/2016/fashion/media/adidas-pharrell-williams-hu-nmd-collection-diversity -261750/.

Wally, Maxine. "The Originals: Pharrell Williams." Women's Wear Daily, November 19, 2018. https://wwd.com/fashion-news/fashion-features/the-originals -pharrell-adidas-hu-sneakers-superstar-exclusive-1202909251/.

Chapter 1: Listening

BBC News. "The Women Who Want to Save Banking." BBC News, May 18, 2009. http://news.bbc.co.uk/2/hi/8048488.stm.

Björk. "Björk on Björk: The Inimitable Icelandic Superstar Interviews Herself." W, October 11, 2017. www.wmagazine.com/story/bjork-interviews-herself/.

Björk. "Stonemilker." Episode 60. Song Exploder, December 27, 2015. http://song exploder.net/bjork.

Boyes, Roger. Meltdown Iceland: Lessons on the World Financial Crisis from a Small Bankrupt Island. New York: Bloomsbury, 2009.

Rees, Paul. "The Songwriters." Q, September 4, 2007. www.bjork.fr/Q-Magazine -The-Songwriters.

Stosuy, Brandon. "Björk on Creativity as an Ongoing Experiment." The Creative Independent (TCI), December 14, 2017. https://thecreativeindependent.com /people/bjork-on-creativity-as-an-ongoing-experiment/.

Tingen, Paul. Miles Beyond: The Electric Explorations of Miles Davis, 1967–1991. New York: Billboard Books, 2001.

Chapter 2: Experimenting

Allan, Jennifer Lucy. "Mothers of Invention: The Women Who Pioneered Electronic Music." Guardian (Manchester, UK), June 17, 2016. www.theguardian .com/music/2016/jun/17/daphne-oram-synthesizer-deep-minimalism.

Fanelli, Damian. "No, Jimmy Page Was Not the First to Play Bowed Guitar." Guitar World, March 21, 2017. www.guitarworld.com/artists/case-you-thought -jimmy-page-was-first-play-bowed-guitar.

Hip Hop History. "Grand Wizzard Theodore (Theodore Livingstone)." https:// history.hiphop/grand-wizzard-theodore-theodore-livingstone/.

Hunt, Chris. "Painter Man: Eddie Phillips of the Creation Interview." Guitarist, March 1988. www.chrishunt.biz/features37.html.

Jones, Josh. "Hear the Only Instrumental Ever Banned from the Radio: Link Wray's Seductive, Raunchy Song, 'Rumble' (1958)." Open Culture, April 18, 2017. www.openculture.com/2017/04/the-only-instrumental-every-banned-from-the -radio-link-wrays-rumble-1958.html.

Palmer, Robert. Deep Blues: A Musical and Cultural History from the Mississippi Delta to Chicago's Southside to the World. New York: Penguin, 1982.

Rodriguez, Robert. The 1950s' Most Wanted: The Top 10 Book of Rock & Roll Rebels, Cold War Crises, and All-American Oddities. Lincoln, NE: Potamac Books, 2004.

Shepherd, John, David Horn, Dave Laing, Paul Oliver, and Peter Wicke, eds. *Continuum Encyclopedia of Popular Music of the World, Vol. II.* New York: Continuum, 2003.

Timberlake, Justin. *Hindsight: & All the Things I Can't See in Front of Me.* New York: Harper Design, 2018.

Turner, Ike. "Rocket 88." Songfacts. www.songfacts.com/facts/ike-turner/rocket-88.

uigvmauricio. "Jimmy Page Guitar Solo Violin Bow." YouTube video, February 13, 2009. www.youtube.com/watch?v=QtoVZ4eObg8.

Chapter 3: Collaborating

Dombal, Ryan. "Beyoncé: 'Hold Up.'" *Pitchfork*, April 25, 2016. https://pitchfork.com/reviews/tracks/18207-beyonce-hold-up/#:~:text=.

Gilmore, Mikal. "Why the Beatles Broke Up." *Rolling Stone*, September 3, 2009. www.rollingstone.com/music/music-features/why-the-beatles-broke-up-113403/.

Inamine, Elyse. "At Loom, Cortney Burns Weaves Together the Threads of Community." *Food & Wine*, December 27, 2018. www.foodandwine.com/travel/restaurants/cortney-burns-restaurant-loom.

Jackson, Harold. "Davis and Dizzy." *Guardian* (Manchester, UK), April 19, 1960. www.theguardian.com/century/1960-1969/Story/0,,105517,00.html.

Lamb, Leah. "Inside the Creative Office Cultures at Facebook, IDEO, and Virgin America." *Fast Company*, August 10, 2015. www.fastcompany.com/3049282/inside-the-creative-office-culture-at-facebook-ideo-and-virgin-airlines#:~:text=.

Peisner, David. "Making 'Lemonade': Inside Beyoncé's Collaborative Masterpiece." *Rolling Stone*, April 28, 2016. www.rollingstone.com/music/music-news/making-lemonade-inside-beyonces-collaborative-masterpiece-85854.

Secret Keeper. "Beyoncé Interview 2018." YouTube video, 11:02. January 22, 2018. www.youtube.com/watch?v=L5wr7fBa27k.

Strauss, Matthew. "Beyoncé's *Lemonade* Collaborator MeLo-X Gives First Interview on Making of the Album." *Pitchfork*, April 25, 2016. https://pitchfork.com/news/65045-beyonces-lemonade-collaborator-melo-x-gives-first-interview-on-making-of-the-album/.

Yoo, Noah. "Ezra Koenig Elaborates on Beyoncé Collaboration, Interviews Ariel Rechtshaid on Beats 1." *Pitchfork*, May 8, 2016. https://pitchfork.com/news/65341-ezra-koenig-elaborates-on-beyonce-collaboration-interviews-ariel-rechtshaid-on-beats-1/.

Chapter 4: Demoing

Aswad, Jem. "Album Review: Prince's 'Originals.'" *Variety*, June 21, 2019. https://variety.com/2019/music/reviews/album-review-princes-originals-1203249946/.

Bengal, Rebecca. "Prince Originals." *Pitchfork*, June 7, 2019. https://pitchfork.com/reviews/albums/prince-originals/.

Carr, Austin. "Apple's Inspiration for the iPod? Bang & Olufsen, Not Braun." *Fast Company*, November 6, 2013. www.fastcompany.com/3016910/apples-inspiration-for-the-ipod-bang-olufsen-not-dieter-rams.

Eames Office. "Norton Lectures." March 31, 2014. www.eamesoffice.com
/scholars-walk/norton-lectures/.

Edison, Thomas. Quote Investigator. https://quoteinvestigator.com/2012/07/31
/edison-lot-results/.

Edwards, Gavin. "Next out of Prince's Vaults: The Hits He Gave Away." *New
York Times*, May 29, 2019. www.nytimes.com/2019/05/29/arts/music/prince
-originals-demo-album.html.

Fassler, Joe. "Jeff Tweedy's Subconscious Songwriting." *Atlantic*, September
16, 2014. www.theatlantic.com/entertainment/archive/2014/09/jeff-tweedys
-subconscious-songwriting/380290/.

Gradvall, Jan. "World Exclusive: Max Martin, #1 Hitmaker." *DiWeekend*, February
11, 2016. https://storytelling.di.se/max-martin-english/.

Greene, Andy. "Radiohead's 'OK Computer': An Oral History." *Rolling Stone*,
June 16, 2017. www.rollingstone.com/music/music-features/radioheads-ok
-computer-an-oral-history-196156/.

Hirway, Hrishikesh. "Wilco: Magnetized." *Song Exploder*, December 2, 2015.
http://songexploder.net/wilco.

Tweedy, Jeff. *Let's Go (So We Can Get Back): A Memoir of Recording and Discording
with Wilco, Etc.* New York: Dutton, 2018.

Chapter 5: Producing

Corben, Billy, dir. *The Tanning of America: One Nation Under Hip Hop*. Four-part
documentary series. Based on the book by Steve Stoute. Produced by Alfred
Spellman and Rakontur. New York: VH1, 2014.

Ferriss, Tim. "Episode 76: Rick Rubin." *The Tim Ferriss Show* transcript. https://
fhww.files.wordpress.com/2018/07/76-rick-rubin.pdf.

Fricke, David. "Jimmy Iovine: The Man with the Magic Ears." *Rolling Stone*,
April 12, 2012. www.rollingstone.com/music/music-news/jimmy-iovine-the
-man-with-the-magic-ears-120618/.

Goldstein, Patrick. "You Too Can Be a Producer!" *Los Angeles Times*, February 20,
2001. www.latimes.com/archives/la-xpm-2001-feb-20-ca-27539-story.html.

Grow, Kory. "Rick Rubin: My Life in 21 Songs." *Rolling Stone*, February 11,
2016. www.rollingstone.com/music/music-lists/rick-rubin-my-life-in-21-songs
-26024/.

Fessler, Leah. "Apple's Top Music Exec, the Man Behind Eminem and U2,
Wants You to Stop Believing Your Bullshit." Quartz, June 16, 2017. https://
qz.com/1004860/jimmy-iovine-the-man-behind-apple-music-and-eminem
-wants-you-to-stop-believing-your-bullshit/.

Sisario, Ben. "Jimmy Iovine Knows Music and Tech. Here's Why He's Worried."
New York Times, December 30, 2019. www.nytimes.com/2019/12/30/arts/music
/jimmy-iovine-pop-decade.html.

Stoute, Steve. *The Tanning of America: How Hip-Hop Created a Culture that Rewrote
the Rules of the New Economy*. New York: Gotham Books, 2011.

Chapter 6: Connecting

Adeigbo, Autumn. "Lessons from Harvard MBA Grad and Feminist Musician Madame Gandhi on Managing a Viral Message." *Forbes*, February 11, 2018. www.forbes.com/sites/autumnadeigbo/2018/02/11/lessons-from-madame -gandhi-harvard-mba-grad-feminist-musician-and-believer-in-the-power -of-periods/#53e0059f5b9a.

Blatt, Ruth. "When Compassion and Profit Go Together: The Case of Alice Cooper's Manager Shep Gordon." *Forbes*, June 13, 2014. www.forbes.com/sites /ruthblatt/2014/06/13/when-compassion-and-profit-go-together-the-case-of -alice-coopers-manager-shep-gordon/#1920def46cc7.

Bourgeois, Jasmine. "Visions: An Interview with Madame Gandhi." *Tom Tom Mag*, November 2019. https://tomtommag.com/2019/11/visions-an -interview-with-Madame-gandhi/.

Braboy, Mark. "Madame Gandhi on the Intersectionality of Feminism and Why 'The Future Is Female.'" *Vibe*, August 22, 2017. www.vibe.com/2017/08 /Madame-gandhi-interview.

Bruder, Jessica. "The Changing Face of Burning Man Festival." *New York Times*, August 27, 2011. www.nytimes.com/2011/08/28/business/growing-pains-for -burning-man-festival.html?pagewanted=3&_r=3&emc=eta1.

Cabral, Javier. "Meet the Man Who Created the Celebrity Chef." *Vice*, November 3, 2016. www.vice.com/en_us/article/aea3v8/meet-the-man-who -created-the-celebrity-chef.

Chakraborty, Riddhi. "Madame Gandhi: The Future Is Female." *Rolling Stone*, December 2, 2016. https://rollingstoneindia.com/Madame-gandhi -the-future-is-female/.

Cross, Alan. "You'll Be Stunned at How Many Songs Are Added to Streaming Music Service Every Day. I Was." *A Journal of Musical Things* (blog), June 12, 2018. www.ajournalofmusicalthings.com/youll-be-stunned-at-how-many -songs-are-added-to-streaming-music-services-every-day-i-was/.

Eells, Josh. "Lil Nas X: Inside the Rise of a Hip-Hop Cowboy." *Rolling Stone*, May 20, 2019. www.rollingstone.com/music/music-features/lil-nas-x-old-town -road-interview-new-album-836393/.

Evich, Helena Bottemiller. "From Daft Punk to Food Labels." Politico, March 7, 2014. www.politico.com/story/2014/03/new-food-labels-fda-kevin-grady -104412.

Fass, Allison. "11 Inspiring Quotes from Sir Richard Branson." *Inc.*, April 10, 2013. www.inc.com/allison-fass/richard-branson-virgin-inspiration-leadership.html.

Fs. "Shep Gordon: Trust, Compassion, and Shooting Friends from Cannons." Episode 65. *The Knowledge Project*. https://fs.blog/knowledge-project/shep-gordon/.

Gallo, Carmine. "5 Reasons Why Steve Jobs's iPhone Keynote Is Still the Best Presentation of All Time." *Inc.*, June 29, 2017. www.inc.com/carmine-gallo /5-reasons-why-steve-jobs-iphone-keynote-is-still-the-best-presentation-of -all-ti.html.

Global Conversation. "Work Hard, Play Hard: The Richard Branson Business Plan." YouTube video, 19:15. January 31, 2014. www.youtube.com/watch?v=g7fbe-oV-X0.

Goodman, Elyssa. "Madame Gandhi Is Here to Disrupt Your Regularly Scheduled Programming." *Billboard*, September 1, 2017. www.billboard.com/articles/news/pride/7949234/Madame-gandhi-feminism-gender-equality.

Lynch, Joe. "How a Bus Driver Changed Madame Gandhi's Life." *Billboard*, October 25, 2019. www.billboard.com/articles/news/pride/8540385/Madame-gandhi-visions-interview.

Kats, Kelsey. "Richard Branson on Start-up Success, Trump and the Time He Drove a Tank into Times Square." CNBC News, July 19, 2017. www.cnbc.com/2017/07/19/richard-branson-talks-trump-start-ups-driving-a-tank-in-time-square.html.

Martin, Emmie. "Billionaire Rich Branson: These Are My Top 10 Tips for Success." CNBC, July 21, 2017. www.cnbc.com/2017/07/21/billionaire-richard-bransons-top-tips-for-success.html.

Myers, Mike, and Beth Aala, dirs. *Supermensch: The Legend of Shep Gordon*. Documentary. Seattle, WA: IMDb, 2014.

One Planet. "Biophilia Educational Project." One Planet Network. www.oneplanetnetwork.org/initiative/biophilia-educational-project-0.

Safronova, Valeriya. "Don't Let Madame Gandhi Distract You." *Paper*, January 21, 2020. www.papermag.com/Madame-gandhi-interview-music-video-see-me-thru-2644883012.html?rebelltitem=15#rebelltitem15.

Thomas, Holly. "33 Years Later, Queen's Live Aid Performance Is Still Pure Magic." CNN, November 2018. www.cnn.com/interactive/2018/11/opinions/queen-live-aid-cnnphotos/.

Chapter 7: Remixing

Biophilia Educational Project. "About Biophilia." https://biophiliaeducational.org/.

Burton, Charlie. "In Depth: How Björk's 'Biophilia' Album Fuses Music with iPad Apps." *Wired*, July 26, 2011. www.wired.co.uk/article/music-nature-science.

Dredge, Stuart. "Björk Cancels Kickstarter Campaign for Biophilia Android and Windows 8 App." *Guardian* (Manchester, UK), February 8, 2013. www.theguardian.com/music/appsblog/2013/feb/08/bjork-cancels-biophilia-kickstarter.

———. "Björk Biophilia App Now out for Android Despite Failed Kickstarter." *Guardian* (Manchester, UK), July 17, 2013. www.theguardian.com/technology/appsblog/2013/jul/17/bjork-biophilia-app-android.

Elektra. "Björk on Telegram." 1997. https://14142.net/bjork/articles/bjork/elektra.txt.

Faena Aleph. "Biophilia: A Revolutionary Educational Project by Bjork." Faena, March 28, 2017. www.faena.com/aleph/articles/biophilia-a-revolutionary-educational-project-by-bjork/#.

Fjellestad, Hans, dir. *Moog: A Documentary Film*. DVD. Written by Hans Fjellestad. Produced by Ryan Page and Hans Fjellestad. New York: Plexifilm, 2005.

Husby, Bård Vågsholm. "Exploring the Dark Matter of Björk's Biophilia Universe: A Study of the Biophilia Educational Project Based on Grounded Theory Methodology." Master thesis, May 18, 2016. Høgskulen på Vestlandet. https:// hvlopen.brage.unit.no/hvlopen-xmlui/handle/11250/2481461.

James, Carmen. "Biophilia Educational Project." Gottesman Libraries, Teachers College, Columbia University, March 1, 2015. https://edlab.tc.columbia.edu /blog/16134-Biophilia-Educational-Project.

Knox, Raven. "Bjork Biophilia." Vimeo, 47:34. October 4, 2013. https://vimeo .com/76167996.

MacDonald, Ian. *Revolution in the Head: The Beatles' Records and the Sixties.* 2nd rev. ed. London: Pimlico (Rand), 2005.

Martin, George. *Summer of Love: The Making of Sgt. Pepper.* With William Pearson. London: Macmillan, 1994.

McGovern, Kyle. "Bjork Needs Your Help to Teach Kids About Science, Technology, and Bjork." *Spin*, January 29, 2013. www.spin.com/2013/01/bjork -kickstarter-biophilia-app-android-educational-program/.

Miles, Barry. *Paul McCartney: Many Years from Now.* New York: Henry Holt and Company, 1998.

Rodriguez, Robert. *Revolver: How the Beatles Reimagined Rock 'n' Roll.* Milwaukee, WI: Backbeat Books, 2012.

Stosuy, Brandon. "Stereogum Q&A: Björk Talks *Biophilia*." Stereogum, June 29, 2011. www.stereogum.com/744502/stereogum-qa-bjork-talks-biophilia /franchises/interview/.

Turner, Steve. *Beatles '66: The Revolutionary Year.* New York: HarperLuxe, 2016.

Wikipedia. "*Biophilia* (album)." https://en.wikipedia.org/wiki/Biophilia_(album).

Chapter 8: Sensing

Aston, Martin. "My Bloody Valentine: Loveless." *Q*, January 1992, 71.

Deevoy, Adrian. "My Bloody Valentine's Kevin Shields: 'I Play Through Pain.'" *Guardian* (Manchester, UK), October 3, 2013. www.theguardian.com/music /2013/oct/03/my-bloody-valentine-kevin-shields-interview.

Dream State(ments). "Control/Surrender: The Gospel According to Brian Eno." *Medium* (blog), July 8, 2014. https://medium.com/dream-state-ments /control-surrender-9b1602a6dacd.

Eno, Brian. "Composers as Gardeners." Edge, July 17, 2020. www.edge.org /conversation/brian_eno-composers-as-gardeners.

Evans, Jules. "Brian Eno on Surrender in Art and Religion." *The History of Emotions* (blog), June 19, 2013. https://emotionsblog.history.qmul.ac.uk/2013/06 /brian-eno-on-surrender-in-art-and-religion/.

Fadele, Dele. "My Bloody Valentine: *Loveless*." *New Musical Express*, November 9, 1991.

Grow, Kory. "My Bloody Valentine's Kevin Shields on the Agony and Ecstasy of 'Loveless.'" *Rolling Stone*, November 15, 2017. www.rollingstone.com/music /music-features/my-bloody-valentines-kevin-shields-on-the-agony-and-ecstasy -of-loveless-204420/.

Jeffries, Stuart. "Surrender. It's Brian Eno." *Guardian* (Manchester, UK), April 28, 2010. www.theguardian.com/music/2010/apr/28/brian-eno-brighton-festival.

Rueb, Emily S. "To Reduce Hospital Noise, Researchers Create Alarms That Whistle and Sing." *New York Times*, July 9, 2019. www.nytimes.com/2019/07/09 /science/alarm-fatigue-hospitals.html.

Wikipedia. "*Loveless* (album)." https://en.wikipedia.org/wiki/Loveless_(album) #cite_note-Tribune_review-70.

Chapter 9: Reinventing

Bienstock, Richard. "Interview: Phil Collen on the Making of Def Leppard's 'Hysteria.'" *Guitar World*, October 1, 2012. www.guitarworld.com/gw-archive /interview-phil-collen-making-def-leppards-hysteria.

Bifue, Ushijima. "Fujifilm Finds New Life in Cosmetics." Nippon.com, April 25, 2013. www.nippon.com/en/features/c00511/.

Fraedrich, Craig. *Practical Jazz Theory for Improvisation*. Winchester, VA: National Jazz Workshop, 2014.

Gross, Terry. "'It Changes You Forever': Lady Gaga on David Bowie and Being Brave." *All Things Considered*, February 21, 2016.

Hammonds, Keith H. "Michael Porter's Big Ideas." *Fast Company*, February 28, 2001. www.fastcompany.com/42485/michael-porters-big-ideas.

Himmelsbach, Erik. "Almost Famous." *Los Angeles Times*, February 5, 2006. www.latimes.com/archives/la-xpm-2006-feb-05-bk-himmelsbach5-story.html.

Huy, Quy, and Timo O. Vuori. "How Nokia Bounced Back (with the Help of the Board)." INSEAD Knowledge, October 10, 2018. https://knowledge.insead .edu/strategy/how-nokia-bounced-back-with-the-help-of-the-board-10211.

Jones, Dylan. *David Bowie: The Oral History*. New York: Three Rivers Press, 2018.

Kot, Greg. "A Glorious Recovery." *Chicago Tribune*, January 27, 1991. www .chicagotribune.com/news/ct-xpm-1991-01-27-9101080478-story.html.

Leddin, Patrick. "What David Bowie's Career Teaches Us About Strategy." Leddin Group, July 2, 2017. https://leddingroup.com/david-bowies -career-teaches-us-strategy/.

Loder, Kurt. "Hysteria." *Rolling Stone*, September 24, 1987. www.rollingstone.com /music/music-album-reviews/hysteria-2-247727/.

Miami Herald Archives. "Gloria Estefan Was on Top of the Music World. It Nearly Ended in Tragedy on the Road." *Miami Herald*, March 4, 2019. www .miamiherald.com/entertainment/music-news-reviews/article227075764.html.

Moreno, Carolina. "What Gloria Estefan Did When She Was Told She Might Never Walk Again." HuffPost, September 12, 2016. www.huffpost.com/entry /gloria-estefan-accident-paralyzed_n_57d6e5bfe4b06a74c9f5d03b.

Nokia. "Our History." www.nokia.com/en_int/about-us/who-we-are/our-history.

Reeves, Martin. "How to Build a Business That Lasts a Hundred Years." TED Talks, 14:47. May 2016. www.ted.com/talks/martin_reeves_how_to _build_a_business_that_lasts_100_years.

Saccone, Teri. "Rick Allen." *Modern Drummer*, March 1988. www.modern drummer.com/wp-content/uploads/2017/06/md100cs.pdf.

Solomon, Micah. "How This New Jersey Factory Is Pivoting Its Business to Manufacture Essential Face Shields in Response to COVID-19." *Forbes*, March 22, 2020. www.forbes.com/sites/micahsolomon/2020/03/22/how-a -private-new-jersey-factory-is-pivoting-its-business-to-manufacture-essential -face-shields/#6433a697234b.

Wagner, Eric T. "Five Reasons 8 out of 10 Businesses Fail." *Forbes*, September 12, 2013.

Warsia, Noor Fathima. "The Essence of Strategy Is Making Choices: Michael E. Porter." *Businessworld*, July 17, 2020. www.businessworld.in/article/The -Essence-Of-Strategy-Is-Making-Choices-Michael-E-Porter/24-05-2017 -118791/.

Wilner, Paul. "Def Leppard's Rick Allen Picked Up His Life—and His Sticks— After a Shattering Car Accident. He's Still Playing, with a Mission to Help Veterans." *Monterey County Weekly*, January 3, 2019. www.montereycounty weekly.com/news/cover/def-leppard-s-rick-allen-picked-up-his-life-and /article_945664b8-0ef9-11e9-83c9-ab395a90e993.html.

Wilson, Mark. "Dyson Plans to Build 15,000 Ventilators to Fight COVID-19." *Fast Company*, March 25, 2020. www.fastcompany.com/90481936/dyson-is -building-15000-ventilators-to-fight-covid-19.

Woideck, Carl. *Charlie Parker: His Music and Life.* Ann Arbor: University of Michigan Press, 1996.

Liner Notes

Thank you Caleb Ludwick, Rick Richter, Todd Schuster, Colleen Lawrie, Kimberly Panay, Ramona Taj Hendrix, Caroline Gregoire, Roger Brown, Berklee College of Music, IDEO, Rita Dalton, Tiffany Knight, Nicole d'Avis, Pharrell Williams, Imogen Heap, Paul Wachter, Tim Chang, Desmond Child, Steve Vai, David Mash, David Friend, Susan Rogers, Justin Timberlake, John Stirratt, Spencer Tweedy, Hank Shocklee, Jimmy Iovine, T Bone Burnett, Steve Stoute, Will Dailey, Kevin Grady, Lawrence Azzerad, André Obin, Jenn Trynin, Kristen Ellard, Kiran Gandhi, Yoko Sen, Emilio and Gloria Estefan, our parents—and all the artists who have inspired us, too many to list!

Hidden Tracks

As kids, we loved finding hidden tracks on CDs. We still do! This last playlist features artists and friends we mentioned in the book, including Michael's musical alter-ego R.M. Hendrix.

SECRET WEAPON, R.M. Hendrix
ORDINARY LIFE, Kristen Barry
TODAY IS CRUSHING ME, Will Dailey
BETTER THAN NOTHING, Jen Trynin
MOON IN THE SKY, Madame Gandhi
NEUROMANCE, Black Plastic
GOLDEN HAIR, André Obin
CREEP (HUNGOVER AT SOUNDCHECK IN BERLIN), Amanda Palmer

Deep Listening: Look for Nirvana's "Endless Nameless," the track hidden on *Nevermind* after ten minutes of silence. See? We're back to the beginning.

Index

Panos A. Panay is senior vice president for global strategy and innovation at Berklee College of Music, the founder of the Berklee Institute for Creative Entrepreneurship (BerkleeICE), and a Fellow at MIT Connection Science. He is also the founder of Sonicbids, a leading platform for bands to book gigs and market themselves online, as well as cofounder of the Open Music Initiative. He has spearheaded multidisciplinary collaborations between Berklee and MIT, the design firm IDEO, and Brown University. Panay has been named to *Fast Company*'s Fast 50 list, *Inc.* magazine's Inc. 500, and the *Boston Globe*'s Game Changers, among other awards and honors. He has spoken about the future of the music industry on programs such as CNBC's Squawk Box and at events such as the World Economic Forum at Davos, Switzerland, and has delivered keynote addresses at events and universities around the world.

R. Michael Hendrix is a partner and global design director at IDEO, a design and innovation consulting firm, where he has worked on everything from home goods to homeland security. His illustrious twenty-five-year career has made him a sought-after speaker; he has delivered design keynotes at *Fast Company*, *Wired*, American Institute of Graphic Arts, Fuse, HOW, and Design Management Institute among others, plus keynotes at SXSW Music. He is also an assistant professor of Music Business/Management at Berklee College of Music and a regular guest lecturer for professional societies and universities across the globe. In his downtime, he writes and records music as R.M. Hendrix.